W9-CFE-995

"Tell me," Matt urged. He could hear the steely glint flash in his voice. Cut the charged tension in the air between them.

"Tell you what?"

He took a step closer. "Tell me that you trust me." His fingers ached to reach out, to take her hand, but Molly looked so scared, so unsure. It was breaking his heart, which was already damaged.

"Tell me that you trust me to do this."

She didn't move when he stood right in front of her, reached for her hands. Taking one of them, he moved it over her stomach, held it there with his. "This is our baby, Molly. You are the most important person in my life, and now there will be two. I will do anything within my power to make sure that you and our baby will never want for anything. Trust that, okay? Trust me."

"I do trust you. I always have." She cupped his face with her free hand. "You really want to do this?"

"Always," he said. "I'm all in."

Dear Reader,

With every book, I forget just how much work goes into creating one. From a nugget of an idea a story is born.

Writing is a solitary beast most of the time, but there is a whole camp of people who are involved in the process, and that's before it gets to you, lovely readers, bloggers and reviewers!

Massive shout-out to my readers, book lovers, and my fellow writers and bloggers in the book community.

To Wakefield Libraries and the folks at Stanley Library, who big me up all the time and are amazing supporters of community, caring and fiction in general.

Huge thanks to everyone on the team at Harlequin for their support, encouragement and patience. I wrote this book suffering from bereavement, COVID and long COVID, and while I despaired it would never be completed, they never wavered or lost faith. Thank you.

Huge gratitude to my lovely friends and family for supporting me, putting up with my clacking away on the keyboard, forgetting dinnertime and muttering to myself.

And biggest thanks of all goes to my readers. Thank you for reading every story and enabling me to write many, many more.

Rachel Dove

A MIDWIFE,
HER BEST FRIEND,
THEIR FAMILY

———

RACHEL DOVE

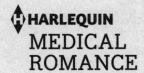

HARLEQUIN

MEDICAL
ROMANCE

If you purchased this book without a cover you should be aware
that this book is stolen property. It was reported as "unsold and
destroyed" to the publisher, and neither the author nor the
publisher has received any payment for this "stripped book."

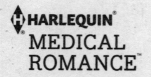

HARLEQUIN®
MEDICAL ROMANCE™

Recycling programs
for this product may
not exist in your area.

ISBN-13: 978-1-335-73784-7

A Midwife, Her Best Friend, Their Family

Copyright © 2023 by Rachel Dove

All rights reserved. No part of this book may be used or reproduced in
any manner whatsoever without written permission except in the case of
brief quotations embodied in critical articles and reviews.

This is a work of fiction. Names, characters, places and incidents
are either the product of the author's imagination or are used fictitiously.
Any resemblance to actual persons, living or dead, businesses,
companies, events or locales is entirely coincidental.

For questions and comments about the quality of this book,
please contact us at CustomerService@Harlequin.com.

Harlequin Enterprises ULC
22 Adelaide St. West, 41st Floor
Toronto, Ontario M5H 4E3, Canada
www.Harlequin.com

Printed in U.S.A.

Rachel Dove is a tutor and romance/rom-com author from West Yorkshire in the UK. She lives with her husband and two sons and dreams of a life where housework is done by fairies and she can have as many pets as she wants. When she is not writing or reading, she can be found dreaming of her next research trip away with the family.

Books by Rachel Dove

Harlequin Medical Romance

Fighting for the Trauma Doc's Heart
The Paramedic's Secret Son
Falling for the Village Vet
Single Mom's Mistletoe Kiss

Visit the Author Profile page at Harlequin.com.

For Auntie Dale Walker
With love

**Praise for
Rachel Dove**

"I found Rachel Dove's interpretation broke that mold and I enjoyed the realistic way in which she painted the personalities. All in all, the well-crafted characters plus the engaging story had me emotionally invested from the start. Looking forward to reading more of Rachel's work."

—*Goodreads* on
Fighting for the Trauma Doc's Heart

CHAPTER ONE

'YOU HAVE GOT to be kidding me.' Molly couldn't believe her ears.

The sign for Ashford Birthing Centre loomed in the windshield, looking resplendent even in the dull January weather. It was freezing outside, and she pulled her black parka tighter around her at the thought. She was glad she'd plumped for her thicker winter tights today. Even in the delivery rooms, where the temperature was controlled centrally, she always felt the cold in winter. A remnant from her childhood, no doubt. Her mother had warmed herself with vodka, and had often forgotten about the needs of her daughter. Sometimes, she still experienced that cold feeling, even when she was wrapped up snug in her adult life.

'What?' Matt looked across at her as he pulled into the car park of their workplace.

His dark brow was raised. 'I only said she wasn't that bad. It was a short ride.'

'Seriously?' Her brows were so far up into her hairline, her whole face tightened. She couldn't help feeling a bit ratty. She hadn't slept well and having company in the car pool with Matt had been a shock, and not a good one. Of all the mornings, and before she'd even managed to get a drop of caffeine into her system. Her flatmate, Amy, had forgotten to buy coffee. 'Next time you give me a lift to work, give me a heads up if you've got someone with you, so I can skip it.' She didn't look at him, but she knew that he was smirking.

'I thought she had some interesting opinions, myself.'

'She was talking about medicine, and the only relevant medical experience that woman has is having a smear test.' She clenched her jaw. 'It was exhausting.' Plus, she never usually saw the women he dated. Not that there were many. Her best friend was not the relationship type. Everyone knew that. 'It just surprised me she was there.'

Matt's tone changed. 'She put me on the spot, and I didn't think. She was moaning about how late she was for work and I had my car parked outside her place. You know I never sleep over normally, but I crashed out.

It was a mistake, an oversight. I thought I was being gallant.'

He had a fair point. What was he supposed to do, say no to giving her a lift? He wasn't cruel to women. Or a player.

'Fair enough. Next time though, I'll get the bus.' She shot him a smile, but he didn't match it.

'No, don't start taking the bus. It's too cold, and you hate the winter. Besides, I like taking you to work. It starts my day off right.' He reached for her hand across the gear stick. 'Forgiven me yet?'

She pretended to seriously consider it. He groaned.

'Mol, come on! You're making me feel like a playboy. I met a woman; we spent the night together. I don't do it all the time. Hardly ever, in fact. It's no different from the dating you do. I just…keep it short.'

'How short?' she quipped.

'Steady,' he warned. 'You know what I mean. Everyone needs a little company sometimes. Even me.' His jaw tightened, and the urge to tease him left her.

She understood that. Throughout her childhood, the one thing she'd encountered was loneliness. It was easier not to trust people, let them in. Relying on herself was the only sure thing. She knew Matt felt the same way. It was one of the reasons she'd let *him* in. Trusted him. She pushed away her intrusive thoughts and focused on her friend.

'I don't think you're a playboy, Matt. I get it. Sorry, grumpy morning.' A phrase he'd coined. He'd learned early on in their friendship that she wasn't a happy little early bird.

He didn't get attached to people, and that's how he lived his life. He didn't lie to the women he spent time with; he was honest about not wanting a relationship. He wasn't like the many men her own mother had dredged up over the years. Or Matt's own father for that matter. The doctor turned lawyer was a world away from him. He was devoted to his job, like her. He had no desire for anything other than what he had.

To be fair, the women all knew the score, even if they sometimes thought they would be the one to finally land Matt Loren, the hot legendary baby doctor. The bachelor with the big family name. His father's work in medical law had seen to that, even before Matt ever picked up a textbook. A high-flying doctor who'd become a medical-professional-suing shark was a difficult act to follow, whether he wanted to or not. The tabloids made sure of that. Some of his colleagues had even judged him for it over the years, afraid he might tell dear old Dad something that would land them in court on a malpractice charge. His dad's record didn't exactly scream trust, and Matt was tarred by association. The things parents inflicted upon their offspring always surprised Molly, even knowing what she knew.

Matt Loren was the obstetrician with a reputation for being cut-throat, at the top of his game. People travelled miles to have their high-risk pregnancies overseen by him.

Women loved all that. You put a baby into the arms of a good-looking man, and it was game over. Ovaries and hearts went all aflutter. If he ever chose to, he could have a woman's company every night of the week. The Loren name was known for producing ladykillers. That little moniker had followed him around in life, even longer than it had at work. Add to it an air of unattainability, and there he was. *Her bestie.*

That's how it usually ended too. The pair of them hanging out. She dated, he had his occasional sleepover, but they always ended up being back to just them. Being confronted by one of his lovers grinning at her from the passenger seat? That felt new, and slightly unpleasant to witness.

'It's fine.' She patted his hand. 'I just wish

you had a bit more respect for yourself sometimes.' He cast her a sheepish look. 'You're a smart guy, Matt. You literally save mothers and babies every day.'

She refrained from adding that his father turning on his original profession and being a player wasn't his fault, and shouldn't mean he be treated the same way. It was true, but he wouldn't hear it. She understood that too. Sometimes, the shadows of their parents blocked out the light of their adulthood. When things grew in the dark, sometimes they grew differently. Harder, stronger. Reaching out for the light with every limb.

She tried not to be mad, but her best friend could be his own worst enemy. 'The least you deserve is a woman who sees that.' She let the smirk she was holding back play across her lips. 'And one who can spell *vagina*.'

'Fair point,' he conceded as they got out of his sleek red Lexus. They headed to the front doors of the workplace they had shared for so long that she couldn't remember a time when he hadn't worked there. 'But I don't exactly ask for a list of qualifications beforehand, Mol. It was only one night.' The second they walked through the foyer, all talk of hookups stopped.

'Busy day today?' Molly asked as they headed to their respective changing rooms.

'Not bad. Liam Evans-Shaw's out for his wedding and honeymoon still, so I have his cases to cover. You?'

'Three inductions booked in. All low-risk.' Molly smiled. She loved the labours that came walking through the doors, but there was something about inductions that she enjoyed more. Probably because the women often came in fed up, their baby overdue, or anxious as hell because they needed to be induced early for one reason or another. Seeing the faces of the parents when their baby was born into the world safely was an amazing high. She had never been one to try drugs or enjoy the buzz of alcohol, but she was addicted to the feeling of creating families. 'Remember the twins I told you about, gestational diabetes? That's today.'

Her patient Emma had had a rough time of it, but today was the day she got to meet her twins. Everything was on track for a double dose of delivery joy, and even the vapid passenger this morning couldn't dull Molly's mood now. She knew her best friend got it. Matt worked the major cases; despite his relatively young age, he was one of the most respected obstetricians out there. He loved the thrill of new life as much as she did.

'Looks like you're buying the first round at Neville's tonight then,' Matt said.

Neville's was the place to be after a long shift, probably because it was near work and the train station. Not too far from where they each lived. Matt had a house of his own, Molly a flat she shared with nurse Amy.

The women were like ships passing in the night though, so it wasn't too bad for Molly. She couldn't afford a place on her own—her disposable income would take too much of a hit. Who wanted to live alone anyway? It worked for them. Amy worked nights exclusively and stayed at her boyfriend Anton's place more than she did at theirs. It was like Molly had her own home, without the crippling expense. It had been a while since Amy was around long enough to hang out with her. She couldn't remember their last night out. Still, flatsharing was perfect for her plan to save some money and pay off her student debt. She'd only had a few months of payments left. Or so she'd thought.

Till she'd woken up to a letter on the kitchen table, kicking her terrible morning off. Amy was sorry to leave Molly in the lurch, but Anton had asked her to move in with him. Marry him. She was leaving at the end of the month.

Since then, Molly had felt the familiar feeling in her gut. The one from her girlhood. Feeling unsettled, askew. Insecure. It was a feeling she despised but could never quite get rid of. Being the only child of a single mum who struggled to be alone, letting anyone and everyone into their lives, who took what they wanted from her and left Molly to pick up the pieces. Not knowing when her next hot meal was coming or when the lights would go back on in the worst weeks. There was never enough money, and her mother had frequently escaped into the arms of a man or a bottle whilst Molly sat at home, planning a future in her head to cope with her reality.

She'd wanted a different life. Her mother never knew her own worth. Molly prioritised hers. She was not someone to be used, cast aside. Those days, those dark memories, they were all fuel for her drive forward. She shunned the shadows and stayed in the light. Her story was not her mother's. She would make sure of it. Having her home life threatened was a trigger she could never cope with easily. Trauma ran deep, no matter how much work she did on herself to combat it. It was in her, part of her DNA.

Even as her stomach lurched, Molly knew it made sense for Amy to leave, and Molly was happy for the friend she loved dearly. She didn't trust easily, kept her circle small. They'd bonded while training and stayed close. Amy and Anton were head over heels for each other. It was the logical next stage for them. As stressed as she felt over the development, she couldn't be mad. Molly would have done the same if she'd been the one lucky enough to be with a man she could spend the rest of her life with. Given her latest dating efforts, finding Mr Right was a million miles away. She would be single and ready to flatshare instead. The whole thing depressed her. She hadn't even had the heart to tell Matt yet.

She probably would have if they'd been alone; he'd have known something was up. Bugged her on the drive to work till she caved. His surprise guest had put paid to that possibility. Besides, she already knew what he would do. What he always did: try to help and cheer her up. She found herself wanting to wallow alone, just a little.

It wasn't only the fact that Amy was leaving. It was the wedding too. A tinge of envy was hidden in her happiness for her friend.

She couldn't help thinking of that old saying 'Why not me?'

Money would be a bit tighter now, that was for sure. She needed to look for another flatmate, but the thought depressed her too much to think about it. By her calculations, even without her flatmate woes, she was still two years off from being able to buy her own place. Put down roots properly. Plus, she had that date tonight. God, she wished she'd never agreed to it in the first place.

She rolled her eyes at Matt as they walked together. 'I can't go to Neville's tonight. Date, remember?'

They headed out of the foyer and stopped outside the doctors' lounge. They did this every morning, usually planning their shifts together and car pool. They were a good team, having started only a week after each other, and the management were more than aware of their skills. They'd become the best of friends. People didn't always get it, but it worked for them. They'd learned to tune the attention on them out. Blur it into the background.

'Date?'

'Yep.'

'Which one is this again?' Matt nodded

distractedly at Shirley, one of the nurses. She simpered back at him.

God, Shirley had been happily married for the past forty years. Everyone in the building either fawned over Matt or declared him the Antichrist. It was like none of them saw the real him. The one that she saw. She brushed the feeling of watching eyes away and focused on picturing her date's face.

'You know which one. The vet.' She blushed at the thought of the evening ahead. Dating wasn't one of her favourite things. It took her a while to warm up to others, and she could spot a red flag from a mile away. Her friends said she was too picky, but she knew what she was looking for. Waiting for it to show up was the problem. In short, she was getting annoyed.

Is it too late to cancel?

No, she thought. He seemed nice. Animal lover, good job. Nice smile. Besides, she'd already cancelled on him twice. Once because an emergency had come in at work, the other time because Matt had dragged her off to watch stock-car racing instead with last-minute tickets. He'd practically hijacked her, but she hadn't been that excited for her date in the first place. To be honest, she'd had a great time with Matt. They'd laughed most of the night. Stuffed their faces with hot dogs and drunk beer from plastic cups. Sat on the sidelines, the roar of the cars and the scent of engine oil all around them. That was a good night, she mused.

She would have to go tonight though. She'd only wallow at home anyway. He *was* nice. She'd bumped into him at the hospital next door. He'd chatted with her, given her his number, asked her out then and there. That never happened! Not to Molly. She wasn't exactly a femme fatale. She didn't think she was ugly, but when she looked at the other confident women out there, she knew it wasn't her thing to get dressed up all the time. She was comfortable just being her, and when she was growing up, her priorities had been different from those of her peers.

With her long blond hair and sparkling blue eyes, she was hardly a Plain Jane, but she was the girl next door type, she guessed. She was more at home in sweats than heels, and that suited her fine. Not every blonde was a bombshell. She was good in her own skin. She just wished, for once, that a man would look at her and think that she was the beginning and ending of his world. When she settled down, she wanted a man who couldn't bear the thought of not being with her.

Hmm, maybe I am a little picky.

She felt a jab in her side and came back out of her head. Matt was leaning against the wall next to her, one brow raised quizzically.

'Earth to Molly. Date? Details? Tell me it's not the guy from Essex.' Matt's voice was flat. 'Tell me it's not Dr Dolittle.'

'Well, he's from Essex, but—'

'Oh, not him—come on! He sounds like such a drip. He puts his hands up cows' backsides for a living. Not sexy. Don't take him back to your place, whatever you do. You'll end up adopting a menagerie.'

'Take him home? On a first date? I'm not you, Matt.' Dating was one thing. Getting naked on the first night? Hell to the no. She was far too nervous for that. She waited till the feelings were there, strong in her gut. Not lower down and regretted later. She crossed her arms huffily.

'Besides, he's a city vet. He deals with dogs, cats, little kids' bunnies. No livestock.' She had no idea why she'd felt the need to defend a date she was suddenly dreading. 'It's only a dinner date.'

Matt shrugged, then pushed himself off the wall and dropped a kiss on her cheek.

'Just be careful, okay? Ring me when you get home like always. Lift after work?'

She nodded at him. He was always playing big brother when she was on a date. They said their goodbyes and got to work. She had babies to deliver, and that always gave her joy. She'd worry about the date later.

CHAPTER TWO

MATT PICKED UP on the first ring.

'Hey! I was just thinking about you. How did it go? Did he bore you to death about animals? It's still pretty early.'

Molly shoved her phone into the crook of her neck, kicking her heels off and flicking them across the wood floor of the hallway. She could hear the TV in the background behind Matt's voice.

'To be honest, boring me about animals would have been preferable to sitting alone in a ridiculously overpriced restaurant. The wine I drank cost more than a full shift at work.'

'He didn't show up? No way.'

'Way,' she huffed, flouncing down onto the sofa. 'And his phone was off. I sat there like an idiot.'

'Are you okay?' His voice was full of concern. 'Want me to knock his head off?' He said it in a mock Essex accent. It sounded comical, but Molly didn't laugh.

'No, no. What's the point? I did cancel on him a couple of times too.'

'Mol, you didn't leave him sitting at a table on his own. What a total fool.'

'Yeah,' she sighed, her eyes taking in the living room for the first time. There were boxes in the corner. Amy had started packing already. Which reminded her of the fact that not only had she been stood up, but she was also about to be minus a flatmate. 'Well, that's my last date. I'm going to buy a house cat and have done.'

Matt's deep laugh reverberated down the line. 'Don't give up, Mol. It's not you; it's him.'

'Is it though, really? I mean, it happens a lot. It can't all be them.'

'It absolutely can.'

'Yeah well, I have enough going on right now. I'm going to give the frog kissing a wide berth for a while. I'll speak to you later, okay?'

'Mol—'

She sighed heavily. 'Matt, I'm fine. Don't worry.'

'What do you mean you have enough going on? What's up?'

'Nothing,' she lied.

Just a bit of impending poverty, or home-lessness.

She didn't want to burden him. She didn't rely on anyone. That was her way. Just because she wanted to find someone to share her life with didn't mean she intended to be any less independent.

'Liar. Spill it, or I'm coming over.'

She could hear his TV click off through the phone, and she knew he was already getting off the couch.

'Sit back down! I'll tell you tomorrow. It's nothing major.' Another lie. She was glad he wasn't in front of her. He could always tell her moods the second he looked at her face. It was extremely annoying. Helpful at work though. Their shorthand with each other was second to none. 'I just want to get showered and get to bed.'

Wash off the stink of rejection.

Matt hesitated, but she knew she'd won. 'If you're sure. Listen, Saturday night. We have the day off together. Let's go out, let our hair down, eh? Bust some of that stress.'

Molly nodded. It did sound good. Matt was a hoot to go out with.

'You're nodding, right?'

She rolled her eyes. 'Yeah. I'm nodding. Night, Matt.'

'Night, Molly Moo. Sleep tight.'

The minute Matt clicked off, she checked her phone for grovelling messages from the vet. Nothing. She threw it onto the couch in disgust. What a night.

Going out on Saturday would help though. She never could handle stress very well. It made her blood fizz like a shaken bottle of soda. She needed to be occupied. Matt knew that better than anyone. He matched her energy. She guessed that was one of the root reasons their friendship had evolved so quickly. Since the first day they'd started working together, his humour had matched hers. Something about him had shattered the ice shield she protected herself with.

She was herself around him. Why couldn't she find that in a guy who wanted to rip her clothes off, make her his one and only? Amy had that. Everyone had that, or it so seemed like it to Molly. Even Matt's dates always showed up.

Sure, he wasn't marrying any of them, but he was still out there. Making connections. At this rate, the only connection she was going to come home to would be one that came with a litter tray and a pooper scooper.

* * *

'You should just move in with me,' Matt said.

Molly was grumpy already, but this wasn't helping. 'Not a chance in hell.'

'What?' Matt stopped the delivery trolley she was pushing with an outstretched hand. The loud squeak it made reverberated down the corridor. 'Why?'

She looked at the clock fob on her uniform pointedly, then crossed her arms with a huff.

He tilted his head. 'Why?' he repeated. 'Just till you get sorted. Renting's not cheap.'

Tell me something I don't know.

'Listen, we need to get ready for the incoming patient. The answer is no, but thanks. I'll be fine.'

'We'll be ready on time. You know that.' He didn't look impressed with her deflection. He was right too. They were like an octopus when they set up together on shift. Fast hands, the two of them working as one and knowing what move the other was going to make every time. A lot of colleagues assumed they were dating when they first saw them together because of how close they were. Matt was a man of few words normally. When they saw him talking away to her, it looked like something was going on. Some of their patients had thought it too.

So they laughed it off. Made a joke of it. Which made everyone else laugh it off too. Sometimes, a little too hard for Molly's liking. As if it was just so alien a notion it was hilarious. Whenever she dared look across at Matt, he didn't look thrilled either.

A bit like now. He was positively pouting.

'It makes sense though. I have the room. You need to keep saving money, and we get on. I don't want you ending up living with some weirdo stranger, and it's expensive to live alone.'

'You manage.'

'Yeah, but it's not cheap.'

Molly rolled her eyes. One thing Matt wasn't short of was money. His expensive car was just one indicator of that. He wasn't showy, but he had his life sorted. The things he did have were high-quality. Built to last. He took care of what belonged to him. 'No, I still have time to figure things out. I will take your brawn if I have to move though. You can help me with that. I'm quite glad actually; I'll be able to get a lot of boxes moved in your penis extension.'

'It's a sports car.'

'Yeah, that's what I said. The phallus you drive.'

'Hey! It's not a phallus. It's special. My dad hated those cars. It's the reason I bought it.'

'Your dad's not dead, and you bought it to spite him because he hate*s* them. Buy a new car.'

Matt puffed his lips together but dissolved into laughter. Only Molly could joke about his dad like that and get away with it. She was the only one Matt ever talked with about him. The Loren publicity machine didn't need his help. His father had sued enough hospital trusts to be notorious in his own right. It had even cost Matt jobs in the past, which had hardened him further. As rigidly as Molly stuck to her independence, her stubbornness and unwavering plan for her perfect future, he stuck to his. His self-imposed isolation from people, hiding the real him behind a seemingly arrogant façade, was a huge part of that.

He wasn't known for being subtle at work. He was used to getting his way. Molly was the exception, and she knew it was frustrating the heck out of him right now.

'Fine but think about it. And don't mock my vehicle. It will be moving all your bits and pieces later. I wasn't kidding though. You could stay with me till you get another place sorted. Like I said, I have the space; you wouldn't even need a storage unit.'

'Oh, yeah, I forgot you lived in a mansion.'

She'd been to his house before, many times. It was a nice detached three-bedroomed house, around twenty minutes from the hospital by car. It was a grown-up house, but that was Matt. He was a goofy guy with a grounded soul. Not that he showed his lighter side to many people.

'It's more than big enough for both of us. Be cheaper than living with Amy, so you could put more aside towards a house of your own. It might be time, with Amy moving on, you know? I know a good mortgage broker, who helped me when Mum... Well, you know. He's a good guy,' Matt pressed.

The prospect of buying a house on her own suddenly seemed like too much work. Something other people managed to do, not girls like her who grew up with nothing. Who were expected to amount to nothing, as if the poor didn't have dreams, or grit. Now it was a goal even further away. A deposit big enough wasn't something she had in the bank right now. She'd only just paid off another chunk of her massive student loans.

She already felt very off-kilter. She needed time to think. Refocus. Not having the most stable childhood really made a difference with credit, and finances. Now that it was all up in smoke, a girl needed a minute. Not to mention the fact that she was still single, with no prospects.

The vet standing her up was just the straw that broke the camel's back. Sure, she didn't need a man to buy a house with, but it didn't mean that she didn't want to one day. She'd always wanted that. The man, the house, the kids perhaps eventually. Once the house was how they wanted it, when they had money in the bank. When their careers were secure for both of them. If she had kids, she wanted to work too, not lose herself. That was important. Her independence couldn't be diminished. Ever.

'Hello? I said are you in?' Matt asked. 'After shift, I could take you to mine so you can check out the spare room? I use the smallest bedroom as my office, but the guest bedroom's pretty big. You can store your stuff in my garage too. It would be cool to have a bit of company.' She was still looking at him agog. He frowned. 'You trust me, right?'

That was never in question. 'Always.'

'Right, so stay with me, okay?' He gave her one last firm 'think about it' look before turning to get to work. 'Till you save up, at least.'

'Why are you so worked up about this? I

looked after myself before I lived with Amy, you know.'

'Yeah, but I know you. Living with some random person would bother you. Better go.' He flashed her a smile.

'I'll think about it,' she yelled after him. He ignored her. He always ignored her. He thought it won him the argument. It probably did, to be fair. She always gave up in the end. Who had time to be mad? She moved on swiftly, didn't dwell on things too long, but always made her decisions carefully. The alternative led to chaos.

'Did I just hear that right?' Adina, one of the other midwives, was just coming out of a patient's room. 'You're moving in with Matt?'

'No. He thinks it's a good idea because Amy's leaving.' The two women fell into step as Molly pushed the trolley towards the other end of the ward. 'Did you speak to your mate from the neonatal ward, the one who was looking for a room?'

Adina shook her head, a rueful smile on her pretty features. 'Sorry. She decided to move back in with her parents in the short-term.'

'Damn it,' Molly said under her breath. She'd asked all of her friends now, having fired off texts to everyone she knew, but no joy. 'I think I'm just going to have to move somewhere smaller, cheaper.'

Adina stopped her before they got to the nurses' station. 'Why? I hate the idea of you being alone in some pokey place. Especially coming off a late shift. Come on, Matt's your best friend and it's better than sharing with some stranger. What's the harm?'

Molly shrugged. 'I don't know. Sharing with a stranger is the opposite of what I want. Unfortunately, I'm stubborn. I just want to stand on my own two feet. Matt will mother me.'

Adina burst into laughter. 'Matt, mothering a woman? That's a first.'

Molly's smile faded. Even her friends didn't understand Matt. It was getting tiring.

'Adina, he's not as bad as you think he is.' Adina's eye-roll told her that her objections were futile.

'Mol, I know you two get on, but you can't convince me that he's not a bit of a tyrant.' The call button went off, and both midwives ran to the sound. Molly never got the chance to refute Adina's claim, and the shift ran on like that all day. None of them had a chance to think about anything else. Mothers came in thick and fast, and she soon found herself happily immersed in her work.

She loved seeing the expectant mothers, seeing their excitement at hearing their babies for the first time. It was the same on clinic days, when she was on that service. Discussing due dates, prenatal care. The joy always rubbed off on her, rejuvenating her from the inside out.

So what if she wasn't one of them yet? She'd meet someone when the time was right. It wasn't over yet. Not till the pregnant lady sang, and she had expectant mothers far past her age who were all doing amazingly well and were equally thrilled to become parents. They had their careers in order, houses, partners. Or so it seemed to her. She supposed most people kept their real fears hidden, just like their aspirations.

Molly just needed to get more ducks in a row, and finding somewhere to call home was the main thing on her mind. It needed sorting, and fast. Before Matt asked her again. And again, and again. Before she caved and moved in with Matt. He was pretty insistent when he had a bee in his bonnet about something and he'd get this little worried furrow on his brow. Become distracted. He always did when she was going through something, which wasn't often.

But she felt his pain too. Usually when his

father was in the news. Another high-profile case. Another triumphant press conference. She hated the look on Matt's face whenever that happened. It stirred something, deep in her gut.

As the shift drew to a close and she headed to the staff-room with the other midwives, Adina's words came back into her mind. She sat down on the bench in front of their lockers and gave her friend the side-eye.

'Adina, you know, what you said about Matt earlier wasn't exactly fair.' Molly bit her tongue. She always got this sort of hot rage burning through her when someone dissed her bestie. Even Liam Evans-Shaw sometimes made the odd joke, and he was Matt's friend.

One glare from Matt and Liam always stopped, but she did pick up on an odd kind of tension sometimes, when they socialised together. From Matt mostly. Like he was afraid of Liam saying something to Molly. It was odd. She'd asked him about it once, and he'd brushed it off.

She sighed, looking at Adina and shrugging her shoulders. 'I don't want to make it a thing, but it's just getting old.'

'What did I say?' Adina thought for a moment. 'The tyrant thing?' She blushed. 'It was a little mean, sure, but he doesn't have the best reputation around here. You must know that. People do talk.'

Molly couldn't deny it. Matt could be surly at work, focusing on his job a little too much perhaps, especially with Liam being off on leave, but he was one of the best too. That didn't come from always being nice and people pleasing.

The tide had turned against him more when an agency midwife had come to cover a couple shifts a few months ago. She'd been one of his conquests, and her criticism of him had got around the centre pretty quickly. Matt hadn't promised her a thing, but when he didn't call her after their one night together... Suffice to say, the old adage about a woman scorned still had legs. And big flapping mouths too.

'Sure, as long as people have tongues in their mouths, they'll talk. But you just don't know him that well.'

Adina raised her brows. 'None of us do. That's the point. The last few weeks he's been downright cold and he was hardly friendly before.'

'Who's hardly friendly?' George walked in, pulling off his ID card from his uniform and using the key on it to open his locker.

'Dr Loren.'

'Oh.' George looked at Molly. 'Well, she has a point.' He clocked Molly's incensed expression. 'Sorry, honey. I say it with love, but Adina's only saying what we're all thinking. The apple doesn't fall far from the tree. Sure, he doesn't sue the pants off people, but he sure scares them off his colleagues.' He smirked. 'And drops a few panties for other reasons.'

'Guys!' Molly shook her head at them, slamming her own locker door and throwing her bag over her shoulder. 'He's not like that, not really. Can we not?'

'Can *he* not?' George wasn't going to back down. 'Don't you remember the Christmas party?'

Molly pulled her jacket off the peg near the door and turned to face them both.

'You mean the Christmas party when he donated all of those toys, out of his own pocket, I might add, and dressed up as Santa?'

Adina had the grace to blush, and Molly turned her glare to George.

'Sure, he did that, but then he didn't speak to anyone but you and Dr Evans-Shaw. He's not a team player, Molly. And we've all heard the rumours about that night.'

'Oh, yeah?' Molly was feeling really angry now. She had heard the rumours. Hell, she'd met a couple of the 'rumours' before. The other morning's car pool debacle sprang into her head, but she pushed it right back out again. 'Enlighten me.'

George sighed, coming over to take her by the shoulders.

'Come on, Mol, we know you two are best friends, but he's a ladykiller, a true Loren; he's arrogant by birth. He gets people's backs up. That's all we're saying. His dad is always in the tabloids. It has to have affected him.'

Ugh. There they go again. Judging.

That was a trigger for her too, and bringing Matt into it sent her heart racing and made her feel increasingly indignant on his behalf.

Molly had had just about enough of people saying things about Matt. They didn't see him outside of work. The Santa thing wasn't a stunt to impress anyone; he didn't even want people to know what he'd done. He was always doing things like that, for Molly, for Liam Evans-Shaw and for his mother, Sarah. If Sarah knew what people thought about her son, she would be so upset.

'I get it, George. He likes the ladies sometimes, sure. What are you, a monk? He doesn't speak to people much, granted.' She looked across at Adina, and she could tell that they'd both made their minds up a while ago. 'Fine,

I'm not going to waste my breath. Matt is a good man; you just don't get him. That's your loss. Bye.'

'Molly!'

'Mols, don't go!'

The two of them tried to block her exit, and she plastered on a smile to keep herself from snapping at her friends.

'Look, I get it. You don't like him, but I do, okay? No point in falling out about it.'

George reached for her hand. 'Sorry, we did gang up on you a bit.'

Molly nodded. 'Yeah, you did. I get it, like I said. I just don't agree with you. If you knew why...' She bit her lip, cutting her own words off. It wasn't for her to say any of that, and Matt would leave work and never come back if he thought anyone knew about his past.

She smiled at her colleagues instead, choosing yet again to take the high road. Sometimes, her friends really were small-minded.

'Listen, I love you both. Matt is not what you think, and he's my best friend, okay?'

Adina raised her brows. 'So, you going to move in with him then?'

Molly let the slamming door be her only response.

Not if I can help it, she replied in her head.

No, she could do this on her own. She headed off down the corridor, knowing the others wouldn't be far behind. She wanted to get out of there.

Matt was waiting for her at the main doors, like he always did when they were on shift together if he wasn't operating or she hadn't been called into a delivery. They always let the other know. Matt had learned she didn't have a car early on and the car pool thing had started not long after. It was about the only bit of help she was glad to accept.

She assumed her best smile to greet him. Seeing him there instantly eased the tension in her shoulders.

'Hey,' he called to her, pushing his muscular body off the stone pillar that was one of two forming the centre's foyer entrance. 'Fancy going for something to eat?' His open smile dropped the second their eyes locked. 'What's wrong?'

She shrugged, irrationally irritated that he'd read her once again.

How did he do that?

'Nothing. Food sounds good.'

His brows were knitted together. The second she reached him, he pulled her in for a hug, drawing attention from their other departing colleagues. She caught sight of

George heading to his car, throwing them an intrigued look that he didn't try hard enough to hide. Molly scrunched her eyes at him, trying to pull out of Matt's embrace. If he noticed, he didn't release her from his arms or acknowledge her actions.

'Matt, come on. People are looking. They talk enough about us already.'

He released her so fast she teetered on her feet. He steadied her, then took a step away and looked around them. His face was like thunder rolling through the clouds.

'Forget about the food, actually. I have to be somewhere.' He was halfway across the car park, keys tight in his fist, before she caught up with him.

'Hey!' She reached for his arm, but he shrugged her off. His phone rang in his pocket, and he grabbed it without looking at her.

'It's fine, Mol. I get it.'

He got it; they both did. It didn't mean that it was any less hard to see him get upset by it. Over time, the speculative looks had died down, but she couldn't move in with him. It wouldn't work. Matt always looked out for her, but she wanted to do things her way. She needed to. It might ruin their friendship, though the pair of them were protective of it. Fiercely. His circle of trust was small too and entwined with hers. They each knew what had shaped the other into the adults they were. Her response was to do things on her own, have control. His was not becoming what everyone assumed he was. Both made life impossible at times.

He understood all that, she knew, but it didn't stop him from trying to help her anyway. That was who he was; he fought fiercely for the people he cared about.

Standing in the car park, she could still see the hurt on his face, even as he spoke into the phone in his hand. He always got angry when people speculated on their relationship. He didn't take kindly to gossip, and with good reason. It was in the air around him so often it choked him.

'Hey, Mum,' he said softly, his gaze looking everywhere now but at Molly. 'Yeah, just got off work.'

He locked eyes with her, and she linked her arms with his, leading him over to his car. He made no attempt to pull away. Their little spat was already forgotten.

'Yeah, Molly's with me.' Molly couldn't make out what his mother was saying, but his frown lines had deepened on his chiselled face. 'Tonight?' He shifted from foot to foot. 'I don't know, I…'

His mother spoke again, faster this time, and Matt seemed to hunch over by a full foot, a deep sigh reverberating in his chest.

'Fine, I'll ask her. Well, she might have plans, Mum—what's the big deal? Okay, okay.' He squeezed Molly's hand into his side tighter. 'We'll be there in half an hour. Love you too.'

CHAPTER THREE

BLOODY GEORGE. On the way to his mother's house, Matt couldn't shake the look the midwife had thrown their way. Even as he thought about how weird it was that his mother had summoned them both to her house at a moment's notice.

He hated that people stuck their noses into his business. Their business. Molly was too nice to see the looks half the time, or she chose to ignore them better than he did. When it got to her too though, he wanted to punch something.

He was well aware of what people thought of him in the workplace, and out of it, and that was all well and good. He liked it that way. Minding their own business, getting on with the job. What they said behind his back he couldn't control, and he'd learned to tune the noise out. They did it whether he reacted or not. These days he tried not to. He didn't

need them to like him. He needed them to do
their jobs to the best of their abilities. When
they didn't, he told them.

Molly was off-limits though, beyond re-
proach, and he would be having words with
George if he carried on like that. He'd be having words with all of them. Couldn't a guy
and a girl be just good friends in this day
and age? He and Molly had never been more
than that. Sure, they were physical with each
other—they hugged and often touched each
other in some way. That was their friendship.
They were like brother and sister.

*No, nothing like brother and sister. Ugh.
No.*

Best friends then. Closer than best friends.
Which was what people just didn't get. She
was his ride or die. He felt his jaw clench, and
Molly's hand covered his on the gear stick.

'Are you going to tell me why we've been
summoned to see Sarah tonight, or give me
the silent treatment the whole way there?' She
squeezed his hand, and he opened his fingers
and wrapped them around hers.

'She just said she wanted to see us both.
It's probably nothing.'

He almost went through a red light, growl-
ing under his breath at the traffic lights.

'Really. That why you're speeding to get

there?' She pulled her hand out of his grasp. 'Slow down.' He headed to the large housing estate his mother lived on, turning onto her street practically on two wheels. 'Matt. She's not sick, is she?'

Matt let his heart start beating again before he answered. The thought of his mum being sick had stopped it momentarily. He'd considered that scenario himself. Her tone of voice had seemed different, off somehow. She never summoned her only child to come over, and asking to see Molly too? His mum loved Molly, but she'd practically demanded he bring her along tonight. Did she know he'd need the support?

'No,' he answered, just to get the look of worry off Molly's face. He'd seen it too much of late. He hated it every single time and battled to keep it at bay. It physically pained him when Molly wasn't happy. His stomach was roiling as he pulled onto his mother's neat driveway. 'Don't worry. It's nothing like that.'

Still, he raced around to Molly's door to open it, then half pulled her out of the car in his haste.

'Okay,' Molly laughed.' I'm coming. I can walk, you know.'

He'd practically carried her to the door in

the nook of his arm. She smoothed his shirt collar down before they walked in.

'Mum?' he called. The house was tidy, like always. He could smell his mother's perfume, and the scent that seemed to be around whenever he was here. The fragrance of home, he mused.

'Hi, you two. Come on in!'

Molly's shoulders dropped to match his as they sagged with relief.

'Well, she sounds happy enough,' Molly murmured. They walked through the hallway to the lounge, and the words of reply died in Matt's throat.

It wasn't the happy engagement banner he saw first, or the group of people who had been his mother's friends for years. It wasn't even the neighbour she'd lived across from for the last twenty, ever since his dad had left them both, and they'd had to downsize to this house to survive.

It wasn't any of that, or the champagne that was being thrust into their hands. It was his mother's face, as she stood there in the arms of her neighbour. With a rather large rock on her finger. For what seemed like an age, the two parties were motionless and stared awkwardly at each other.

'Oh, my God, Sarah! Congratulations!'

Molly had been holding his hand, and as she rushed forward, his hand followed her for a moment. She tried to tug him along behind her, but he felt rooted to the spot. The whole room was all smiles and chatter, Molly exclaiming over the ring and hugging the happy couple. Matt felt like his face was on fire. He felt Molly come back over to his side, linking her arm in his. It broke him from his stupor.

'Wow,' he said through barely unclenched teeth. 'Congratulations.'

He managed to sit through the niceties. The neighbours and friends around them kept up the chatter. Molly thrust a plate of food into his hand at one point, and he ate reluctantly. He would much rather have gone for a curry with her like he'd originally wanted to instead of being trapped in this nightmare. He had managed to move away from the crowd and was staring at the wall of photos up in the conservatory when Duncan found him.

'There you are,' he said jovially.

Matt took his time looking away from the smiling faces behind the frames to acknowledge the interloper. 'Here I am,' he retorted. 'Standing in my mother's house, wondering why I was the last to know about you two.'

He finally turned to face the man who had

been his mother's friend for years. When the scandal had hit and his father had left them for the secret family Matt and his mother had no clue about, they were broken. And broke. He'd stripped the accounts, and knowing the law, he'd been sneaky about hiding his assets too. Taking him to court wouldn't have done them any good. Not even if they could have afforded it. Mutual friends had shunned them. Crossed the street to avoid them, either not knowing what to say to them, or being too much in Mr Loren senior's thrall to break ranks and check on the family he'd left behind. It was astonishing to Matt, even now, how people with money could do whatever they liked. His father's PR firm had handled it like a dream, burying the bad news. His other woman was introduced to the media like a new date, and they ate it up. The 'new' family were made respectable overnight. His first one cast out, left to fend for themselves.

They'd moved out of the area from unwarranted shame and financial necessity. He'd never forgotten how shattered his mother was. How long it had taken for her to crack a smile again.

When they'd first moved here, to Kent, to this decent, understated street, Duncan had been the one to show them kindness. Now

Matt felt like that kindness might all have been a ploy. Had it?

Duncan, to his credit, didn't bite. He walked over to the drinks trolley in the corner and poured two stiff Scotches into crystal-cut tumblers. Matt felt his jaw flex. Those tumblers were one of the few things from their old life that they'd managed to hold on to. Seeing them in the other man's hands made him feel a pang of grief. Duncan was standing in front of him now, offering one of them. He took it, nodding once towards the comfortable overstuffed sofa, and the two men sat.

'I didn't want to keep this a secret from you. I know how close you and your mother are, but it was her decision. I had to respect that. Tonight's celebration was sprung on us really. You know what your mother's friends are like. They got a bit excited.' He looked sheepish as he said the next part. 'I understand that you're protective over your mother, and why.'

Matt felt his anger rise, but it wasn't at Duncan. It was at the last man she'd got engaged to. Married.

He wasn't a man. An amoeba, more like.

'It was a shock, that's all.' Matt looked across the room at the man who had made his mum happy again. He wasn't oblivious. 'I know she's been a lot happier lately. I guess I just didn't think too hard about why.' He had been distracted by work, been busier than usual. Molly's flatmate moving out was worrying him too. Molly still hadn't sorted anything out, and he knew she was stressing about it. 'How long?'

Duncan didn't look away. Matt respected him for that. 'It was purely friendship at first. When you guys first moved in across the street, I just wanted to help. You were only small. You had to grow up a lot faster than the other kids in the neighbourhood. I hated seeing that. I wanted to be there, for both of you. It was company for me too.'

Matt knew all that already, but he let his impatience fade. Let Duncan finish. He was a good man. Before tonight, he'd always really liked him. Duncan had taught him to fasten his first tie. Even given him driving lessons in the supermarket car park after it was closed. He'd taught him many things that his own father had never been there to do. He'd been glad that his mother had company when he'd moved out, to go away to study to become a doctor. It had always given him comfort. He didn't want her to be alone. So why did he have such an issue with this now? Why did everything seem like it was changing? He suddenly felt out of his depth.

There was movement near the doorway. Matt saw a flash of material. Molly's light blue dress. He looked up, and could see that she was hovering, out of sight. Or so she thought. It made his lip twitch.

'I get that you've been there for Mum as friends, but this is something else entirely. I never had a problem with you being part of our lives.'

'But you do now?' There was a noise in the corridor. A little cough. 'Matt, your mother is a grown woman. She knows what she wants, and I love her. Dearly. That woman is all I care about. My sole purpose in life is to put a smile on Sarah's face. Without her, I just don't function.'

Matt heard an 'Aw...' from outside the door, clear as a bell.

Duncan kept his face straight, but Matt could see his eyes flick towards where Molly was hiding. 'I think you might understand that too, not that you'd say as much,' Duncan continued. 'Take a few days—that's all I'm saying. Let it sit. You know where I am when you want to talk. If you need to. Just know that I will never come between you and your mother. You can count on that.'

Matt stood, and Duncan stood with him. 'I love my mother, and of course I want the best for her.' He ran his free hand down his face before offering it to Duncan in the form of a handshake. 'Congratulations, Duncan. I know you'll make her happy. I just might need a minute to process.'

Duncan's whole body relaxed, and the two men shook hands.

'The offer's there. Just knock on my door, anytime. Your mother is my life. I was put on this earth for her. I know it in my gut.'

Matt's mind threw an old childhood memory at him, when he'd had trouble with his bike. He'd knocked on Duncan's door then. They'd fixed it together on his driveway. He owed the man respect, even if the news was still jarring. Before Matt turned to leave, Duncan said something that ran circles in his brain for hours after they'd left the party.

'I think you'd have your own reason to exist if you'd only let it happen, Matthew.'

The two men patted each other awkwardly on the back before Duncan slipped out to find Sarah.

'Come in here, earwigger,' Matt said, loud enough for Molly to hear. She poked her head around the door a half second later.

'Oh, hi!' She looked around as if she'd just

been dropped from nowhere. 'I didn't see you there.'

Matt rolled his eyes. 'You are a terrible liar. You came in case I knocked him out.' Her lips twitched with amusement, making the corners of his own mouth turn up.

'Well, that or bundled him into the boot of your car, never to be seen again.' She came to give him a hug, and the tension in his shoulders dropped away as he wrapped his arms around her. He drained the rest of his glass and dumped it onto a side table. 'He's a good bloke, you know. Sarah's always singing his praises.'

He pulled away to look her square in the eye. 'Did you know?'

She shrugged, her nose scrunching up in her signature way. She looked cute when she did that. He bopped her on the tip with his finger, and she wiggled it back at him.

'I've had a feeling about them for a while.' She waved her hand towards the photos. 'They're in a lot of photos together. They go on days out. They're always together, they hang out, go shopping. They don't date anyone else.'

'You just described us,' he pointed out, and it made him think of Duncan's final words.

Molly looked away. 'Yeah, but I don't date

much because I'm broke and have no social life, and you don't date because the big C-word terrifies you.' Looking back at Matt, she said, 'It's a bit different.' She hugged him tighter, and he lifted her off the ground till she laughed out loud. 'We're best friends. Nothing will change that, will it?'

She wriggled out of his grasp, flashing him her best smile before heading off to say goodbye to Sarah and Duncan. As Matt followed her out, he couldn't help the feeling of unease that sizzled in his gut. He was never good with change; it always made him feel out of control. Trapped even. He couldn't shake the feeling that something momentous was about to happen, and he once again wasn't in a position to stop it. The boulder was already rolling towards him, and he had no option but to wait to be crushed.

'Hey.' Molly's blond head bobbed back around the door. 'You coming, or what? I'm still hungry. Let's get a burger on the way home.'

Matt smiled, letting her pull him along by the arm. Anything for Molly. Ride or die.

CHAPTER FOUR

It HAD BEEN a week from hell, and Molly could not wait to let her hair down. Work had been hectic, she'd had no joy in looking for a flatmate, or a cheaper place to live, and she was starting to panic. Every time she went home, Amy had boxed up more of her stuff, and the place was starting to look derelict.

She'd never had much, never needed much really. She'd left her mother's house with the clothes she'd been wearing and hadn't looked back. Her mother's parade of boyfriends was not something she'd missed. Once she'd got into university digs, even having three flatmates had made for a much less chaotic household than the one she'd left. Now, after she'd found Amy and had such a nice, easy time with her, the uncertainty of where she was going to live, and with whom, made her really anxious.

She'd spent the day looking through listings, ringing around the rest of her friends to see if she could get lucky, but things were not looking good. When it came time to get ready to meet Matt, Molly was already a stiff glass of Merlot in and itching to go somewhere.

They normally ended up hanging out on their time off. Movies, nights on the town. Bowling. It had been a while since their last proper night out. Too long. She'd been so busy saving up, and with Liam off work getting hitched, Matt had been pulling a lot of extra hours. A good party for the pair of them was long overdue.

She took her time on her make-up, and even raided Amy's wardrobe for a dress with a little bit more zing than she usually wore. Since she was in her uniform at work and in her sweats when she wasn't, this felt like an opportunity to really go all out. Give the old confidence a boost after the vet debacle. She wanted to feel hot for a change. Kick her heels off and have some fun.

She chose to go smoky-eyed, red-lipped and skilfully applied eyeliner to make her blue eyes stand out all the more. She surveyed herself in the mirror. The look was dramatic against the blond of her hair, which she'd curled for a change. She looked like a different woman. It was eerie what a bit of make-up could do to a person.

'New make-up, new hair.' She smiled into the mirror. Amy was normally a lot more daring in her wardrobe choices than Molly was. Growing up, Molly'd always had rent to pay, books to save for. She didn't spend her student loans on going out, or fancy things. She had neither the spare money nor the inclination to waste what she *did* have. She felt like that plan was faltering, and the young girl who'd had no control was screaming at her from the inside. Warning her to keep working harder. Rise over the speed bumps. It was exhausting worrying about it all. Worrying that she was heading for a disaster.

Tonight, she wanted to feel different. After thumbing through the dresses Amy hadn't packed yet, she'd selected a gold dress, one that shimmered like silk and clung to her curves. She'd never been a skinny girl; she'd always been a little voluptuous with curvy hips. Her mother called it her hourglass figure. She'd mostly hidden it under her uniform and comfortable baggy clothes that served a purpose. She'd always been so conservative, so functional. In contrast, her mother had used her looks to get what she wanted till they faded with vodka and the passing of time. Molly had learned early on to dull her shine. It wouldn't do to outshine the narcissistic woman who'd birthed her. Trauma was an education, and some lessons were hard to unlearn.

She'd realised since Amy had told her she was getting married that she'd been holding her own life back. She was so used to playing it safe, wanting a life so far away from her upbringing. Striving to get it at the expense of living sometimes. She envied how settled Matt was despite the family dynamic he'd grown up in. Having one awesome parent was something she'd never experienced first hand.

He had a home ready for the family she wanted to have one day. She was still trying to make her home, and the irony that he didn't want any of that for himself wasn't lost on her either. She was sick of watching other people live their lives whilst she just tried to plan hers and hope nothing derailed it.

Well, tonight she was going to forget her troubles, and just live in the moment. Matt was the perfect drinking partner for that. All he did was live in the moment. He worked hard, played hard. Kept life fun. Looked out for himself. That was what she needed to do. Perhaps tonight she'd ask him how to do it.

Pushing her tired feet into the nude heels

she'd splurged on, she checked her reflection in the full-length mirror in the hallway next to the front door. Still her, just more. It gave her a thrill to see how great she looked. She might even turn a few heads in the club tonight. She took a photo on her cell phone and sent it to Amy, who was already at work for her night shift. She'd be starting soon, but she texted back right away.

Wow! You should dress like that more often! Have fun, babe! Love ya!

Amy was one to tell it straight. If she said that Molly looked good, she could trust it. Everything was set for a great night out.

'Wow, Mol, you look...'

Matt's face was a picture when he came to pick her up in the taxi. She jumped in, shut the door behind her and shoved her clutch purse onto the seat between them.

'Different? Sexy?' she offered, laughing at his expression. He was like a fish out of water, gasping for breath.

'Very sexy,' the taxi driver butted in, leaning back over the seat.

Matt snarled the address of the first bar at him, and the driver concentrated on pulling away from her flat at speed and heading towards town.

'Well, he approves. What do you think?' Molly giggled, shimmying her shoulders at him.

Matt's scowl deepened.'I think you need a jacket.' He turned to gaze out his window, moving his body away from her.

'Wow, well thanks, Matt.' Molly flinched and shrank back into her seat. 'I thought I looked good.'

She instantly felt his hand under her chin, holding it between his fingers and pulling her to him.

'Sorry, Mol. You look great. It was just a bit of a shock, that's all.' He lowered his gaze, and she could feel his eyes appraise every inch of her. 'You look amazing. That's a dress and a half.'

She grinned; his odd response forgotten instantly.

'Excited for tonight?' he asked, changing the subject. 'I must admit, I can already taste my first pint.'

'I can't wait.' She smiled back. 'A night out with the doctor—just what I ordered!'

The first bar was already pretty busy. The outdoor seating area was lit up by lanterns and electric heaters around the tables. Matt was at her door before she had a chance to open it, and she heard a wolf-whistle as she stepped out onto the street in front. Matt took her hand in his, and walked her in.

'I see we're in for an interesting night, with you wearing that,' he said, his face paling slightly as he fully took her in. 'I might just start on the whisky instead.'

She swatted at him playfully with her clutch, heading to the bar. Secretly liking his protective streak, which seemed to have sharpened with her outfit choice. 'Come on, grumpy. First one's on me.'

Four drinks in, they were sitting in a booth at the back of a small bar called Passion. They'd spent most of the night messing about, dancing to the music, making each other laugh. It's how they were whenever they went out. They had so much fun on their own, they didn't need anyone else. Molly was feeling buzzed from the drinks, and Matt had steered them to a quieter place to catch their breaths before hitting the clubs.

'So what's with the different look tonight anyway?' Matt looked at her over his glass.

'I felt like a change, that's all.'

A little bit of rebellion against my anxiety.

'Well, you accomplished that. It feels like everyone's changing these days.' He looked like he wanted to add more, but he took a sip of his drink instead.

She changed the subject, though she didn't throw it far. 'Including your mother getting remarried?'

'Touché.' Matt's lip twitched. 'Yeah, in a way. Liam's married now, Amy's getting married. Mum and Duncan—I mean, I didn't see it coming but I can hardly stop it. I don't think I would if I could. I don't have to like it. I just worry about the fallout, I guess. Old habits. I want her to be happy.'

'You always want your mother to be happy. Who says there's going to be a fallout?'

Matt drained his whisky, eyeing the bar.

'Not so fast.' She knew him too well. He was wanting to escape the conversation. She'd seen him pull that move a lot over the years. 'No more drinks till you tell me what's happening. Is it because of your father? Do you think he knows? About your mother I mean.'

Molly watched Matt change from mildly irritated to downright shut-off in the space of thirty seconds.

'I couldn't care less what he knows. It's none of his business. He gave up that right years ago. It's everyone watching him, us.

Getting picked over by the gossip mill. I just worry for her, that's all. I need another drink.'

She reached for his hand, but he was already gone. Stalking off to the bar, glass in hand. She watched him walk away, his shoulders up around his ears, and found herself hating the man who had abandoned him. The legendary Phillip J. Loren. Matt had always felt like he was in his shadow, but Matt just didn't get that he already surpassed him in every way. She wished more people could see what he did at work. How good he was with his patients, with her. His mother. Liam, who had pulled strings to land him the job despite Matt's infamous surname.

He was special, but the front he put up often made him look and sound like a jerk. People saw his chiselled appearance, so close to his father's, heard his surname, and connected the two. Combined with his aloof attitude and thanks to that loose-lipped agency nurse, everyone thought he had a rotating door of girls on his arm. They assumed he was cut from the same Loren cloth. Treated him as such. No matter how much Matt differed in reality.

Scandals had a habit of sticking to people. Even the rich who could pay the best spin doctors. His father's two daughters and second wife were never dragged through the papers. Matt was incensed at the fact that people compared him to his parent. Wrote him off before they knew him in person.

He could never live like that. Two families, two homes. It had changed Matt for ever. Molly could see the tension in his shoulders when he walked away, the pressures getting to him. He was twice the man his father was, but he just didn't see it. Which made him almost as stupid as everyone else who thought badly of him.

Even her own colleagues had denounced him, and they did know her. Why would they think she would hang out with the man they described? They made him sound like a cross between Scrooge and Mr Darcy. They thought she was foolish for being his best friend, but Molly was loyal. Fiercely. Especially when it came to Matt. She knew from her own experiences not to judge people on rumours and hearsay, or what their parents did or didn't do. If people associated her with her mother in such a public way, she knew she'd fare just as poorly. Anonymity had a lot of comfort hidden within.

She was so busy stressing about her own situation, she'd barely thought about how Matt might be feeling. She wanted to make it right. Reclaim the fun of the night. She was about to follow him, to have it out with him and clear the air, when her line of sight was blocked.

'Hey, gorgeous,' a man drawled, his words slurred. 'Having a bad night?'

'No, and I'm waiting for someone.' Molly was trying to look over his shoulder to track Matt, but the guy wasn't having any of it. He moved closer, leaning over the table and knocking into the glasses. She pulled one back along the table before it got smashed to the floor. She hated drunk people like this. It reminded her of the good-for-nothings her mother would bring home sometimes late at night.

'Oops,' he said, laughing like a hyena. 'I saw your guy. Seemed a bit moody to me.' He leered, looking her up and down in a way that made Molly feel decidedly uncomfortable. She could see his mates, all three sheets to the wind themselves, egging him on from a distance. 'I could treat you better.'

'No thank you.' Molly went to get out of the booth, purse in hand, when the man blocked her exit, sitting down next to her.

'Aww, come on. Play nice, eh?'

She wiggled as fast as she could to the other end of the booth. It was getting pretty busy now, and she looked around for someone to claim the moron. His friends just grinned at her.

'Sorry, love. He's harmless. He just got dumped,' one of them, probably the least drunk of the party, shouted across at her. 'He fancies you, blondie!'

'Wonderful,' she shouted back in a retort, before putting her purse in between herself and the man. 'Go enjoy your night with your friends. I'm not interested.' She might as well have saved her breath. He wasn't listening to a word she said.

'Come with us! You'll have a much better night with me, eh?'

His hands were already lifting from his sides as if to grab for her.

'Hey!' she shouted, but then she saw Matt loom behind him. He put the drinks he was holding down on the table, fixing the man with a cold glare.

'You heard her. Move. Now.' The bloke stood up and pirouetted on his unsteady feet, turning to look up at Matt, and Molly used the opportunity to squeeze by him. Drunk and Dumped's friends came over like flies round garbage, surrounding Matt. He tucked Molly into his side, shielding her with his body.

'Hey, man, what's your problem?' one of

them asked, and Drunk and Dumped kept talking to Molly like nothing had happened.

'So, you coming with us? We're going to Shooters next.' Shooters was a bit of a dive bar. Patrons could play pool there after hours, if they didn't mind their feet sticking to the decades-old carpeting. She'd dragged her mother out of there enough times to know never to set foot in the place ever again.

'I said no. Matt, let's go.'

Matt shook his head, pointing to the drinks he'd just bought. 'No need. These guys are leaving, and we're going to finish our drinks.'

He fixed the men with a look that Molly hadn't seen often. He was shaking with suppressed anger, she realised. She could feel it reverberating through his arm as she slipped her hand into his. He squeezed it tight.

Drunk and Dumped followed her arm movement, his face turning from hopeful and tipsy to sozzled and bitter in an instant.

'Oh, I see. Like that is it?' He thumbed in the direction of the doors, missing by a mile. 'Come on, lads. She looks like a bit of a ho anyway.'

One second, the man was standing there. Well, swaying. The next, he was barrelling backwards, right into his friends. He felled his mates like bowling pins, drinks flying up into the air and smashing down around them. Molly saw Matt uncurl his fist, leaning forwards and pointing his finger right into the man's face.

'Don't you ever speak to her like that again,' he growled, his other hand still in hers. She tried to pull away, but he gripped her tighter. He turned to her, looking her up and down. 'Are you okay? You get hit?'

She shook her head mutely, not quite believing what had happened. Matt scowled back at the men, who were busy picking each other up off the floor.

'Come on, Matt. People are looking. We need to go.'

She managed to pull him away, and soon they were heading through the bar and out onto the street. The second they were outside, she pulled away. He let her go this time.

'Molly, stop.'

She kept walking, away from the crowds, towards the top of the street where the taxi rank was. Her heels were pinching the hell out of her feet, but she kept on. The night air was hitting her, making her feel the alcohol in her system. She was never normally a big drinker. A couple of shots and she was tipsy, but her anger was fuelling her on.

'Molly, stop!' he repeated.

'No,' she spat back. 'Why did you hit him? If he calls the police, that's it for you. No more job, no more career. What the hell was going through your head?'

'He was going to put his hands on you! That's what was going through my head. He had no right to talk to you like that. I just lost it!'

She huffed and kept walking.

'Molly, stop please. I can't fall out with you. I hate it. Stop. Please.'

She'd already started to slow but hearing the plea in his voice stopped her dead. She turned to face him, and he strode over. Took her into his arms. She went willingly but gave him a tap on the arm to express that she was still irritated with him.

'Ow!' He rubbed his arm, though she knew he didn't even feel it through his muscle. He was in the gym far too much to be hurt by a slap.

'You deserved it. You keep playing into people's hands. He was just drunk.'

'Who needed a good telling off.'

'Yeah,' she retorted huffily. 'Not a punch in the face.' He grunted in response. 'I mean it. I defend you all the time, but sometimes...'

He sighed heavily, and she felt his chest rise and fall under her cheek. She listened to his heartbeat, still racing fast from the adrenaline of the past half hour.

'I know, I know. I'm sorry. I just didn't like it. I didn't think.'

'You were in a mood even before that when you walked off.' She felt him tense in her arms.

'I wasn't.'

'You were,' she rebutted. 'That's why you flipped, isn't it?'

He sighed. 'I know that it was my fault the creep got near you in the first place. That's why I got so mad. I shouldn't have walked away.'

'Fair enough.' She could see what he was saying. He was her best friend. If anyone had done that to him, she'd have probably wanted to let her fists fly too. 'It's not down to you to protect me or stay glued to my side but I get it. It's over now.'

'It won't happen again because I won't be walking off next time.'

Molly puffed out her cheeks. 'I don't think dressing like this is going to be something I repeat.'

'Yeah?' He kissed the top of her head. 'Well, that's a shame. I kind of like it. You were confident, more than I've ever seen you before. Don't let those idiots tonight spoil it for you.' He pulled away to look her in the eye. 'You deserve to be looked at, looked after. I just didn't want you to get hurt. The thought of that man touching you...'

She shushed him and pushed her finger against his lips. 'Come on. I'm fine. It's over. Let's just go home.'

'Oh, no!' Matt tried to pull her back up the street towards the clubs, but Molly dug her heels in. Literally. She planted her stilettoes against the kerb and crossed her arms. 'Mol, don't let my stupidity ruin our night. We don't have to go to a club. We could try Jenkinson's—it's normally pretty dead at this time.' He checked his watch, waggling his brows at her by way of challenge. 'You never told me how the housemate hunt was going.'

She waved him off. 'You didn't miss much. I'm still searching, but it's looking like I might have to move instead.' She shivered. 'I don't want to talk about it right now.'

He tapped his shoulder. 'Broad, you see? Problem shared...problem halved.'

She bit her lip, wondering how much she could tell him. Even with Matt, she kept some things close to her chest. He knew that she and her mother didn't speak any more, that they didn't have the best relationship even before that. She didn't know herself why Amy's leaving and getting married had stirred her up quite so much, but it was really doing a number on her. Leaving her anxious, unsettled. Antsy to change her life in ways she had never thought about before, and frustrated because she couldn't.

'My heels are killing me,' she said instead. That was a truth she could willingly share. He looked down at her nude stilettoes, nodding once. 'I'm not really in the mood to party after that.'

'Right. My place it is then. I have a liquor cabinet ready to be pilfered.'

She shook her head. 'I should get home.'

'To an empty place?' His brow raised theatrically. 'Amy's out for the night. You'll just sit and stew about things. Come on, we can stick one of your favourite films on.'

'*Predator?*' she checked. She was never one for romance movies. In her mind, *Predator* was more likely to happen than some of those romcoms ever were. She could never see anyone running through an airport to declare their love for her or standing up in a wedding chapel to stop the ceremony going ahead. Hell, even in her thirties she'd never been lucky enough to date a guy she'd even consider going up the aisle with.

He groaned at her request. They'd already

watched it. A lot. '*Predator*, really? How about we compromise with *Die Hard*?'

Molly thought for a moment. She'd already made him watch the Bruce Willis movie last month at Christmas, but she didn't remind him of that. 'Throw in a takeaway pizza, and you have a deal.'

Matt scoffed, but she knew from his smile that she'd already won. They headed to their favourite pizza place on the way, and as they ate the slices, sitting on a bench waiting for their cab, Molly realised something. That whatever she was going through, heck, whatever the two of them were going through, they at least had each other. Nothing would change that. It was about the only thing besides her job that she could bank on.

'I love you to bits. You know that, right?'

Matt smiled, his lips glistening with the grease from the pepperoni under the street lights. 'I know. I love you too, Mol. You and I against the world, right?'

She bumped her arm against his playfully. 'Right.' She grinned at him. 'Always. At home, at work. Everywhere.'

'That's good to hear.' Matt's jaw clenched, a sombre expression dulling his features. 'I think George hates me, and the others aren't exactly friendly these days. I know I've been extra moody lately. I've been overdoing it covering all Liam's work and it's made things worse.' He smiled at her, but it fell flat. Molly's heart clenched, like it always did when she saw her friend looking sad or lost. He was like a boy when he looked like that, not the arrogant man he projected to everyone else.

She had a sudden thought as she sat there eating, and it grew to take over all the other thoughts in her head. Maybe it was the alcohol talking. She never drank much, and she was feeling the effects a little now, even with the food in her stomach. She felt brave. Naughty, perhaps. She had just had a man defend her honour against an unsuitable suitor. That was hot, even if Matt was the one doing the defending, wasn't it?

Whether it was the adrenaline or the dress, she didn't know, but she didn't stop herself from talking for once.

'You know, when you first started at the centre, I said something to George about you.' Matt's eye-roll made her laugh. 'Don't roll your eyes at me. It was nice, I promise.'

'Yeah, well, it didn't work. I don't think he's my biggest fan.'

Molly finished her last slice and wiped her hands on one of the napkins she'd snagged from the restaurant counter. 'He's harmless.

A bit judgemental maybe, but harmless. No, it was when you first started. I was new too, of course. I'd been there a week, and everyone was excited about the new doctor coming.'

Matt rolled his eyes again, but his lips bore a slight smile. There was no arrogance on his features; he was almost bashful about how good a doctor he was behind closed doors. The rest was bravado, and skill never let him down. Never made him a liar. She and Matt were both young, ambitious and at the top of their game.

'Is there a point to this, or are you just blowing smoke?' He took a napkin from the bench between them and wiped at his mouth.

'Yes, there is. Let me talk, okay? No more eye-rolls.'

He blinked to stop himself and fell silent.

'Well, I was a bit frazzled that day, and when I walked into reception, I walked right into you.' She didn't expect any recognition to cross his features. He hadn't taken any notice of her then. He'd never seen her that way. Not like she'd first seen him. She hadn't always looked at the man and automatically thought 'best friend' material. 'I remember we were busy that day. Loads of little things needed to be done. We were in a flap. I was taking

some donations from the local library up to
the wards, a bunch of—'

'Knitted hats,' he finished for her, his tone
quiet. 'I remember. They fell all over the
floor. The box crushed right up between us.'

Molly's voice gave out on her for a second.

*He remembers? Well, he remembers the
clumsy oaf with the hats. Of course. Not the
slightly erratic blonde behind them.*

'That's right. Anyway, you helped me to
scoop them up, put them back in the box.
You were wearing that dark grey suit I used
to love on you.' He was staring right at her,
their thighs close enough to touch. She felt
a little awkward now she'd started her story,
but she wanted him to know. She'd come this
far. She could take a little embarrassment to
cheer her friend up. 'Well, George was at the
nurses' station when I got back. He asked me
why I was so flustered, so I told him. I'd just
met the man of my dreams, right in the foyer.'

She looked away, feeling the blush hit
her all over again. 'I swear, I gushed about
you for half an hour straight. Me!' She was
laughing now, recalling how she'd talked and
talked about the jolt she'd felt when their fingers touched, how cute she thought he was.
Something about him had told her that he was
special, and Molly wasn't the kind to tell any-

one her feelings. She usually made it a habit not to have them.

'I was such a lovesick puppy, George was jumping up and down on the spot, and then you walked round the corner. Doctor's jacket on, Liam showing you around, and I realised who you were.' She shook her head at her own stupidity for declaring all her feelings out loud back then. 'I never told George it was you to this day. I was too mortified, and I would never have heard the end of it.' She giggled again. 'Can you imagine if he'd known it was actually *you* I fancied?'

When she glanced back at him, she expected him to be laughing too. Ready to take the mickey out of her, like he always did. He wasn't laughing. He'd gone pale. His eyes were fixed on hers, as if he was searching for something.

'Oh, come on,' she mumbled, suddenly feeling awkward. 'It's not that bad, is it?' He looked positively downcast. It stung her. A lot. She might not be his usual type of woman, but she was good enough to be his best friend, right? Was the thought of her fancying him that repellent?

She brushed off her dress, getting to her feet. 'You don't have to worry. It passed pretty quickly.' She turned away from him, buying time for the sting of humiliation to fade from her features, when she set eyes on him again. Even her outfit felt stupid. Wrong.

Who am I trying to kid? I'm the friend, the girl next door. Not the one that men would set their world on fire for.

'Come on, there's a taxi just pulled up.'

'Why didn't you tell me?' He was closer than she thought. Standing right behind her. She turned to face him. He was inches away from her. She felt his warm breath on her cheek. His expression was incredulous. 'Why didn't you tell me you liked me? I didn't have a clue.'

Molly played it off, the embarrassment having burned away the rest of the alcohol buzz.

'What, so you could get a big head and tease me for ever? No chance. I only told you tonight so you'd know that not everyone hated you on sight.' She slammed those shutters right back up. 'I need to go home. My heels are killing me. See me to the taxi?' She wanted to go back to her flat, get rid of the awkward moment between them. With a bit of luck, he'll forget this by morning. Things would snap back to normality. She didn't get to the taxi before his arm was linked through hers.

'Bruce Willis, remember? You're coming to mine.' They were both in the cab before she could protest, and he fired off his address to the driver before Molly could blink. The taxi pulled out onto the road and drove off into the night.

'Are you going to be weird about this?' she asked, talking to the back of his head. He'd been looking out of his window as if he wanted to climb through it. 'I only told you to make you feel better. I thought you'd laugh. George never knew it was you, if that's—'

He whirled around in the back seat, his eyes pinning hers.

'I don't give a damn what George knows. That's…that's not it.' He was coiled, she noticed. Tensed up tight.

'Well, what is it then? I told you; it was a passing thing. That's all. I wish I'd never said a word now!'

'But why now?' He was raising his voice with every sentence. 'Why wait all this time? I've… Oh, God, Mol. I…' His face was pale, as if he was running their entire friendship through his mind with this filter of new information layered over it. 'I really wish you'd told me.'

'Yeah, well, I wish I never had!' Her shields intensified around her. 'Forget it. Just take me home.' She tried to look away, but he stopped her.

Matt's hands were on her face, his fingers gripping her gently. 'I can't forget it, Molly.'

'Yeah?' she breathed, trying and failing not to feel the tension between them. The shocking frisson of sexual charge that filled the back of the cab and crackled around them. 'Well, I'm asking you to forget it. I'm telling you to. It was—'

'Don't.' He stopped her, a warning tone in his voice. 'Don't pretend it's something I can ever forget, Molly.' His gaze dropped to her lips, and she felt the pull of him like she never had before.

Tonight had been different from the first moment he'd seen her... She'd felt this before now, she realised. It wasn't the first time he'd watched her this evening. While her mouth wrapped around her straw, when she laughed. She took him in, removing the best friend label from him. Just for a second. To see...

All the touches, the hugs, the up-close dancing. It had never felt like this between them, except when there had been a crushed cardboard box of knitted hats between their bodies. Somehow, they were so close in the taxi that not even that box would have squeezed through. His chest was warm, his breathing hard. Matt, the man. The man she'd fallen for in the foyer years ago. It was as if he was suddenly right before her. Like the first time she'd seen his face. She'd shut those feelings off, but they were back in full force now. Screaming at her through every nerve ending. She felt like she was on fire. He inched even closer.

'Try,' she said, but it sounded feeble to her own ears. 'Forget everything I said tonight.'

A half second before his lips crushed down on hers, she heard the growled response reverberate from him. 'I will, if you can forget this.'

She didn't answer. She kissed him back, and they clung to each other.

CHAPTER FIVE

THE AIR HAD changed around them. Even when they were out of the cab, she could still sense it. Fizzing anticipation. Matt paid the driver, passing him too many notes and not bothering to wait for change. He took her by the hand, saying nothing till his front door closed shut behind them. Molly could feel the electricity as he dipped his head to hers once more. Walked her into his house with his lips. For a half second, before he pushed her against the wall of his living room, she swore she saw a spark jump from his flesh to hers.

This is Matt, Molly. Your best friend. Get a grip!

'Matt,' she breathed, half a question. Half a plea. 'What are we...?'

'Don't think, Molly.' His gruff voice cut the rest of her objection short. 'Let me kiss you.'

She could do nothing but look back at him. His expression was something she'd never witnessed before. Not first hand. Not even second hand, come to think of it. He was looking at her like he wanted to absorb her into himself. Her lips went dry.

'Let me,' he said, so slowly, so deeply it felt like a low rumble reverberating across her skin. Her whole body felt hot. The dress she'd worn for her night out was tight, but now it was uncomfortable. Restricting. She could feel her nipples harden painfully against the balconette bra she'd scaffolded them into earlier. She wanted to rip it off, relieve the pressure. 'Molly, let me make you feel good.'

'Matt…'

She wanted to tell him he always did that, that he didn't need to do it this way. Not for her. Even if she did feel like she might burst if she didn't escape his grasp. Hell, she wanted to run home and furiously pleasure herself.

It wouldn't be the first time.

Right now, she needed to leave. Go home. Purge the urge to ride her best friend like a rodeo bull. She was tipsy, but not drunk enough to be able to play it off afterwards. She had to stop it now.

'Can I kiss you?' he rasped.

This was a bad idea wrapped in a pulsing bag of nerve endings, and *oh, oh, oh…* He was kissing her face now. She realised she'd whispered yes at him. He'd wasted no time, a ghost of a smile crossing his lips before he put them to work on better things. Dropping seductive kisses on her cheeks, trailing his five o'clock shadow along her skin.

'Molly, tell me what you want.' His voice was husky and utterly sexy. She wanted to record it, to save it for ever. Replay it every day for the rest of her life. He stopped kissing her, fixing her with the eyes she knew as well as her own.

She tried to look away, pretend she didn't know exactly what he was talking about. And what she wanted her answer to be.

Matt was having none of it. One hand on her hip, he held her steady against the wall. She could feel his body shaking against hers, his groin pushed against hers so deliciously it made her eyelids flutter. His other hand reached up to grip her chin between his fingers, his eyes devouring her like he had been waiting to do this since the moment they met.

'Matt, I think…'

His whole body went rigid the second she spoke. He didn't draw a breath. He was waiting for her. This was her opening. She needed to shut this down, now. While she still had control of her faculties and her sexual urges, while their friendship was still intact enough to laugh this off. She should say something, anything.

She parted her lips and spoke the truth. 'I want you to kiss me.'

His full mouth sealed onto hers, and her thoughts vanished. Everything vanished. The Earth fell away around them, and Molly didn't think to mourn the loss of any of it. What she had in front of her now was worth the loss. God, it was worth it. Every coherent, independent thought fell straight out of her head, replaced by a surge of lust that roared through her. Her moan was stolen by his mouth, and he growled in response.

Is this what Matt was like with those other women?

She pulled at his shirt.

'Do you want me to stop?' he half panted, his eyelids hooded. The black lashes she'd always coveted fanned around his piercing blue eyes. 'Molly—'

'No,' she sighed. 'Don't stop.'

She shut down any thoughts of other women feeling this, feeling him, when his hand curled into her hair. He wrapped her locks around his fingers and pulled, gently but insistently. Her neck tilted to one side, willingly, hungry for him. Hungry to get the full Matt experience.

My Matt.

His tongue glided down the line of her jaw, and he nibbled at her earlobe, sending a hot shiver running through her.

'Need more,' he mumbled, dipping his head to suck at her collarbone while she wrapped her fingers tighter around his shirt, pulling him closer. He grunted in frustration, not able to lift her dress higher than an inch around her thighs. 'Hold tight.'

She was in the air, his arms around her waist as he turned and strode towards his stairs. He lifted her till she was straddling him, his large, masculine hands strong around her as they ascended. He kicked his bedroom door open, then slammed it shut again with his foot and deposited her on her feet. She was here, in his bedroom. She'd been in here before, so many times, but in this moment the atmosphere crackled like wildfire. She stood before him, feeling oddly naked and exposed. Her whole body burned with anticipation and incredulous shock as she met his gaze. Saw his eyes rove over every inch of her. How was this happening? She'd never felt so sexy in front of a man in her life. She was soaked, and desperate for her best friend to put his hands on her.

'Tell me to kiss you again, Mol.' He leaned

in, touching the zip fastener at the side of her tight dress. It made a tinkling sound against the thick gold ring on his thumb. She'd bought it for him one birthday. 'Tell me what you want me to do.' Again he waited for her response.

'Take it off,' she demanded.

He gripped the fastener between his fingers and whooshed it down to the bottom. The fabric pooled like a shimmering gold rose around her bare feet, and she felt a slight chill from the air in the room. She didn't remember when she'd lost her heels. Her nipples squeezed painfully tighter, so aroused now she knew that Matt would be able to see it. Feel it.

'Hell,' he muttered. His face lit up at the sight of her skimpy matching underwear set, and she was suddenly glad she'd made the effort tonight. 'How did you go out like that? If I'd known...'

He kneeled before her. She watched him take her in, his sky blue eyes roving lower till he'd run over every inch of the scant fabric covering the last of her modesty. He drifted a finger along the edge of the lace, making her breath hiss in through her teeth.

'Tell me you don't wear these in my presence at work,' he said hoarsely. 'I would never have got a thing done had I known.' He lifted his gaze, locking his eyes on to hers as his index finger dipped under the seam of her thong, branding a hot line of sensation right against her sex.

Oh, my God. Now I'm imagining him in the OR, bending down over me, taking off his scrubs and...

He hooked his fingers under each side of the thong and pulled till the scrap of soaked material was at her feet. She went to step out of them, and he stilled her. Standing, he slowly walked her backwards till the backs of her legs hit the edge of the bed. The panties stayed where they were, and her bra soon followed its partner to the floor.

She waited, watching him as he watched her. Both of them standing there, her naked, his chest rising and falling sharply as he took in her nude form. She should feel embarrassed, self-conscious. This was Matt. Her friend Matt. It should feel strange, but she couldn't stop staring at his rapt expression. He looked like he'd always wanted this with her.

Had he?

She did, she knew. She'd buried it well, sure, but she couldn't deny it. Not while standing naked before him. She wanted him badly.

'You are stunning,' he exclaimed, a happy little smile playing across his intent face. 'I always knew you would be. Tortured myself with it.' She wanted to ask what he meant, but his eyes had grown dark, less soft. He dipped his head to drop a kiss onto her lips, and that's when all hell broke loose. It was as if everything had sped up. Fast, so fast. So hot. She kissed him back, just as hard. They were a mess of teeth and tongues, lips and hands. He went to lift her into his arms, but she put both hands on his chest and pushed.

'No,' she said, breaking the kiss. He stopped immediately, looking stricken. His face turned so bleak at the loss of her touch, it thrilled her. Surprised her and totally turned her on.

'No?' he echoed, breathing hard. 'Molly, I—'

'You have too many clothes on.' She smiled at him devilishly, enjoying the look of intense relief on his face. It soon turned to lust when she put her fingers on the buttons of his shirt. 'Let me help you, Doctor.' His lips twitched. 'I feel like we need to even things up.'

He stood there, watching her intently as she went from the bottom of his shirt to the top. One pearly-white button at a time. She reached the top of his chest, pushing the material aside, and he gasped as her fingers ran down his muscular front. She'd always known he was ripped; she'd seen him in both boxers and swim shorts before. They were always comfortable around each other, but now she was touching his body in ways she never had. Running her fingertips down the contours of his abs, enjoying the feel of his taut skin, the way he stilled under her touch. He was holding himself back; she could feel the sexual tension within him. He felt so good, so—

Matt growled. An honest to goodness throaty, wolf-like growl. The second she'd touched the waistband of his trousers, reaching for the belt buckle, the sound had come out of him. Dragged from his throat as if she'd pressed a button on his groin. His lips crashed down on hers again, and she hopped up to wrap her legs around his waist this time. He took her in his arms as if she weighed nothing, pulling her to him tight, and then lowered her onto the bed. He stepped back only to finish what she'd started. He removed his belt, threw it to the floor and kicked his trousers aside.

Desperate for him, she watched him with a hungry gaze. He was hard, and he'd gone commando. Having sprung free of his pants, his shaft grazed his belly. It was swollen, and he pumped it a couple of times as if he couldn't bear the pain of his desire. She expected him to join her on the bed fast, quick. He surprised her by lying down slowly, hovering over her and caging her between his arms and legs. She could feel his length press against her stomach as he kissed her. This time, it was slow. Much slower, tender even. He took her face between his hands and kissed her like a man who'd arrived safely back from battle would kiss his true love. She kissed him as long as she could before the want of him became too much.

'Matt,' she panted. 'I want you.'

She still couldn't believe that this was happening. They'd been drinking, but they were far from drunk. She knew what she was doing, and the reality of it felt far away. Something to think about later. All she could think about now was him being inside her. Feeling every inch of him.

He pulled back, sitting up and taking her with him.

'Are you sure?' he asked, his eyes intent on hers.

'Yes,' she breathed. 'God, yes.'

He went to say something else, then bit

his lip. A habit when he was thinking something over, but she didn't want him to think. She wanted action, and she knew that Matt could deliver.

She reached for him, and took him in her hand, running up and down his length. He hissed, releasing his lip and reaching shakily into the nightstand. A moment later, he was ripping the wrapper off a condom. He didn't take his eyes from hers as he sheathed himself. She moved for him again, and he kissed her back down to the mattress.

'You're so beautiful, Mol. My Mol.' He was whispering to her between kisses, moving from her lips to her jaw, dipping down to kiss her nipples. One at a time, slowly. Taking one into his mouth while gently pinching the other. She was writhing beneath him on the sheets, trying to touch him, but he kept moving away. Teasing her.

'Let me touch you,' she begged. He shook his head, coming back to cage her with his limbs again.

'I need a minute,' he confessed, and she realised he was shaking. 'I want this to last. I need this to last.' He looked a little sad for a moment, and she wanted to ask why but he silenced her question by sliding his hand down between their bodies. He ran his finger along her centre, triggering what felt like lightning against her nub. He moaned, almost as loud as she did.

'God, Mol, you're so wet,' he breathed as he moved his thumb in circles around her core. 'So soft.' He was touching her with the rest of his fingers, gliding them from side to side, as his thumb moved in every direction. It was delicious and dirty in equal measure. Molly was beside herself with lust, her eyes so lidded she could barely see straight. 'I can't stop touching you.'

'So don't,' she whispered, pulling him down to kiss his face off. She wanted to get her fill while she could. Before reality and the morning kicked in. Before the last of the alcohol burned out of their systems. 'Touch me, Matt. I want you so badly.'

He groaned again and shifted his weight. Molly could feel the tension in his muscles and wondered how it would feel if he let go. Really unleashed the power he was holding back. She wanted it all. Every little bit of it. She could feel the tip of him now against her. Ready to push in, to take her, and she couldn't bear it. She needed him now. She grabbed his firm butt cheeks with both hands, pulling him closer.

'Mol, wait— I—'

'What?' She stopped, her hands stationary on his body. 'What's wrong?'

He was looking down at her. The light from the street lamp outside was coming through the open blinds. It shone in slants across them both, across the sheets. She could see the conflict in his features, and her blood went cold.

Is he regretting this already?

She went to move, to leave, but his hands were around her in an instant.

'Nothing's wrong.' He shifted back, just a fraction of an inch, giving their bodies the tiniest bit of space from each other. Fixing his baby blues on hers, he smiled. 'I'm just glad you're here. With me.' He pushed a lock of hair back from her face, and then there was no more space between them. He moved slowly, the tip of his hardness resting against her entrance, before he thrust forward. They groaned together at the sensation as he slowly filled her. Inch by wildly sexy inch.

'Holy hell,' he growled. 'Can you feel that?'

'Well, if I said no, I'd be lying.' He stopped to look at her, and they both laughed.

'I didn't mean that,' he said, before thrusting again. Molly moaned, wrapping her arms around his shoulders. 'I meant how it feels.' He pulled back, teasing her with his hips before entering her again. 'Can you feel that? Tell me, Mol. Tell me how good it feels.'

He was almost needy, his intent gaze watching her every movement. He slowly built up the pressure, touching her all over, kissing her, stopping to tease her and suck at her neck. Molly's whole body was on high alert. She felt so seen. Worshipped. His eyes roved over every little centimetre of her. His hands couldn't stop touching her.

'Tell me, please. I need to know,' he begged.

She could feel herself melting. She felt like she was turning to liquid in his arms, her pleasure growing and threatening to take her and everything around them with it in a gigantic explosion. She had *never* been so turned on. Her head felt hot, white-hot. She was starting to shake with the force of her feelings.

'So good,' she said, gasping out a feeble description. 'You feel so good. So hard. I can't take it.'

'Yes, you can,' Matt rumbled back, his voice coming from deep in his chest. 'I want you to feel everything. All of it.' He thrust, harder, his movements becoming less defined. More erratic, ragged. She could tell from the strain on his face that he was trying to hold himself back, and it turned her on all the more.

'Why haven't we done this before?' she asked, pulling him tighter as her orgasm built. She could feel it, on the cusp of overflowing within her. His thumb came between them, pushing and twirling, his hips thrusting and his lips claiming hers, and she came in that instant. Hard and fast. She came with such force she bit down on his shoulder to stop herself from screaming out loud.

'God, Mol, you're so damn hot. Molly, I—'

Her orgasm still ripping through her, she clamped down on him. Her hands gripping his body, pushing him into her firmly and giving her everything. Hell, she didn't think that she would ever get enough, and she wanted him right there with her. Always.

He came within seconds of her, a low, almost visceral groan rumbling through him as he shuddered inside her. Deep and needy. 'Molly. God, Molly. Damn.' One of his hands was clutching the cover, knuckles white. She'd heard a rip of material somewhere along the way to their bliss.

They were both breathing heavily, the aftershocks still running through them both. He kept kissing her, not stopping till they were both down off their cloud. Till their wildly pumping hearts settled into a normal rhythm again. Till they stopped feeling the other's beat against their chest. The room grew silent.

Matt kissed her nose and propped himself up on his elbows. 'Beautiful.' He had a look on his face Molly hadn't seen before. Like he'd finally figured out the key to life.

His post-sex face looks like that? No wonder no woman ever wanted him to leave.

She could see the attraction now. She would find it hard to forget this, she knew. To go back to being just his friend. It was like seeing the other side of life, just once, before moving back to the grey normality of the day to day.

'Wait right there. Don't move,' he said, and she watched his retreating naked form as he left the bedroom. A moment later she heard the bathroom door open, the toilet flush. His feet padding down the carpeted stairs. Him moving around, the soles of his feet hitting the tiled kitchen floor. Before she could regain her senses, he was back in the room. He had two cold bottles of water in his hands, and he offered her one. He pulled the soft navy blue comforter from its folded position at the bottom of the bed, covering them. He made no move to dress, check the time. They both drank, and Molly found she was thirsty.

Her lips felt swollen, bee-stung. They'd been kissing for what felt like hours, but she knew from the light of the street lamp that it wasn't yet morning. She felt like days had passed and they were only two people in the world. Like time and work were all irrelevant now. Only this was what mattered. Being here, together. In the afterglow of what they'd just done.

The water drunk, he took the bottles and put them on his bedside table. Reaching for her, he lay on his back, tucking her into his side. Pulled her close, kissing the top of her head over and over. His arm kept squeezing her tightly to him, and she laid hers on his chest. Running her fingers over the lines of his body lazily.

'I should go, let you get some sleep.' She knew he was playing football in a few hours. He played for his local team when he was off shift. She often went to see him play. The other lads had thought she was his girlfriend at first. She wondered what they'd think now if they saw her again.

'Don't be daft,' he murmured in the dark. Beneath her ear. 'Sleep here. Stay with me.'

'We didn't watch the film.'

'Who cares? What we did was better than any film, Mol.'

She thought of all the times they'd been in his house. Not one of them had been like this. Next time she was here, would she be able to stop the feeling of disappointment? When he hugged her to him, would she want more? She knew what *more* meant now. What it felt like. A line had been crossed tonight. She was one of his groupies. She'd told him as much, how she'd fawned over him the first time she'd met him. Then this had happened.

She'd seen her mother do it often enough. Fawn over a man, get him into bed. They never stuck around. She was always alone, or worse. Broke. Dependent on the next man who smiled at her. Now Matt was more than a friend. She'd broken her own rule. It was going to be messy. So messy. He was the one man she did trust, but this was well out of best friend territory.

She felt him shift, moving closer and turning to face her, both of them sharing the same pillow. Her head lay on his arm as he cradled her. He twined his legs through hers.

'You're quiet.' He was running his fingers up and down her arm. Tiny little touches. It was very distracting. 'Are you okay?'

'Tired,' she lied.

'Really?' he pressed, his brow cocked. 'That's it?'

'Shocked,' she admitted. 'I didn't see this coming.'

'Me neither,' he replied. His face had that expression again. He looked serene...at peace. Like he'd figured something out. 'I didn't expect it at all. Listen.' His hand stilled in its movements. 'Molly...'

'I really am pretty tired,' she said, yawning. She needed time to process things. She knew the score. Matt didn't do attachments. She wasn't under any illusions. She'd messed up. She was looking for the man to father her children, to share her life with. Matt wasn't interested in doing that with anyone. Nothing could come of tonight, and now the consequences of their actions had started to hit home.

She knew the score but had chosen to ignore it for those few glorious hours. She wasn't ready yet for him to give her the speech. It was a one-off. She was in agreement on that one at least.

The alcohol and adrenaline of the night were catching up with her, and she felt her eyelids grow heavy. 'Let's get some sleep, eh?'

Something flashed over Matt's face.

How will our friendship survive this?

She felt sick just thinking about it.

After a long moment, he nodded his head. 'Turn over?' he asked, and she rolled away from him. Her back to his front, she felt his arms encircle her again. Caging her with his arms and legs and warmth.

She felt safe, and cosy, like she always did in his embrace. But she also felt like she was going to cry. What the hell was she going to do? Everything was messed-up. She'd opened her big mouth, and out had wriggled a huge can of worms.

'I'm glad you're here, Mol.'

She didn't answer. She didn't know what to say, so she kept her eyes closed, choosing not to fight the tiredness.

CHAPTER SIX

'I'M GLAD YOU'RE HERE, Mol,' he said to her in the darkness. He found he couldn't stop the words from coming out now. She was naked and warm, wrapped in his arms and legs. His limbs were all around her, keeping her safe.

She didn't answer him, but she shifted slightly in his embrace. Closer. He took it as a sign to continue on. He felt like a sap, but the floodgates were open now. All along she'd liked him. The first time she'd met him, she'd deemed him worthy to be with her. He still couldn't believe his ears. He'd wanted to shake her, demand why she'd never told him before now. All those times they'd been close, and he'd thought he'd spotted a glimpse of something between them, only to brush it off. Everyone seemed to have a comment on the two of them. His patients thought that they were together all the time. Molly would just roll her eyes and make light of it. He did too.

It still hurt like a dagger though. He'd never imagined he'd be good enough for her.

When they'd finished making love, he'd felt cheated. Like he'd had a taste of something sweeter than he'd ever dreamed, and it was already over. When she'd turned over like he'd asked, it was easier to tell her. Hide, without her eyes focused on his. He'd always lost himself in her gaze.

'I wish you'd told me.' Once he started, he didn't stop speaking. He had to get it out. Had to speak his truth into the dark of the night. Chase the shadows of unsaid things away for once. 'I remember that first day. You crashed into me, and I was just…hooked. You took my breath away. Winded me too.' He smiled at the memory.

She had been dressed in her midwife's uniform, tiny woollen hats all around her. Her blond hair was tied back, functional for work. The dark shade of her uniform brought out the blue of her eyes. When he'd first set his sights on them, he'd forgotten everything else. That blue had been his favourite colour ever since. The cardboard box was smashed between them, the integrity of it crumpled. A bit like his heart, which had cracked open a little that day too, just enough to let her wiggle her way inside. She'd never left since.

'I wanted to talk to you, but I was already late. It was my first day, and I was due to meet Liam and the rest of the team.' Molly stayed quiet. He could hear her breathing. Even, relaxed. Secure in the embrace of his body. 'I wish I'd just asked you out there and then.' He'd wanted to. Badly. Even if his brain told him that this woman wasn't a one-time thing.

'By the time we talked next, it felt like a bad idea. I didn't want to make work complicated.' He sighed, mad at himself again just remembering his reluctance. He was always so driven, so focused on work. 'I figured I would keep my distance. Get on with the job.' He'd tried, but that had lasted about half a day. She was too friendly, too much a part of the place to avoid. 'We became friends, and I figured that was the next best thing.' He kissed the back of her head, pulling her closer even though they were already wound together. He could never be too close to her after this.

'Till tonight. I still can't believe it, to be honest.' He chuckled to himself. 'Maybe Duncan had a point. I think he hinted at this the other night.' She didn't answer. 'What do you think?' She didn't move. He leaned over, looking down at her face. She was fast asleep. 'Mol?' She didn't stir.

'Damn it,' he muttered. He'd poured his heart out, and she'd missed the whole thing. After dropping another kiss onto her cheek, he settled down next to her. 'Never mind. There's plenty of time.' He smiled to himself in the dark, his best friend in his bed, in his arms. 'All the time in the world.' He thought of all the ways he could deserve this woman. To keep her. He thought of his mother, starting out again. Happy. In love. Perhaps things changing weren't so bad after all. He fell asleep, holding Molly tight. After tonight, he was starting to think that it might be worth a try. His Loren heart had hope for the first time, and he wasn't in a rush to let it go.

Matt was still smiling when he woke up. The sunlight streamed through the open blinds, casting shadows on his face and making him squint. It took him a moment to realise that something was amiss. He'd been dreaming, him and Molly together as always. Laughing, messing about. Kissing. His arms were empty. He looked around him, but he was alone in bed.

'Molly?' he called. 'Do you fancy going to breakfast? I'll skip the footy.'

He pulled himself out of bed, eager to see her. As he put some boxer shorts on, he noticed that Molly's clothes were missing from his bedroom floor. Well, he could hardly expect her to walk around naked. He pulled his robe off the back of the door, stuck his arms through it and headed down the stairs. 'Molly?'

The house was quiet as always. Too quiet. He went into the kitchen but stopped dead when he saw it empty. 'Mol?' he shouted, listening intently. She wasn't here. He turned and ran back up the stairs two at a time. His mobile phone was still in his trouser pocket from the night before. Maybe she'd nipped home to get changed.

Why didn't she wake me? I'd have driven her.

He went into his bedroom and was just bending to pick up his trousers when he saw it. He'd missed it before, but he couldn't take his eyes off it now. An ominous feeling ran through him. Crawled up his spine. He picked up the folded piece of paper from the bedside table. His name was written on it in Molly's familiar swirly handwriting. He opened it with trepidation. Molly wasn't usually one for notes. But she'd left without waking him. He wasn't stupid. He'd left a few sleeping sexual partners himself. No notes, but still. He held his breath, hoping she was just telling him she'd be back soon. She'd gone to get coffee, breakfast. When he read the note, all hope left him.

Matt,
Thanks for last night! It was fun! See you
at work, mate.
Molly x

Mate. She'd friend zoned him in a note. She'd skulked out before he woke up, dashed off a quick scribble. *Fun! It was fun?* He sank down onto the bed, reading it over and over. It was so…offhand. Banal. Cold even. Not his Molly. It didn't sound like her. She'd acted like it was just one of their usual nights out together. It was anything but. She'd told him about her crush. He'd opened up to her. She'd been asleep, but still…

He thought of them last night, him kissing her like his life depended on it. Holding her. Making love to her for the first time. For the first time with her, and the first time ever. He'd never had sex like that. Never wanted a woman so badly, and not just with his body.

Did she really not feel any of that?

Her actions said it all. He'd said it himself. *Let me make you feel good.*

He'd offered himself to her like some

kind of happy pill. She'd taken it that way.
He thought back to their conversations. She'd
never said anything back, had she? She'd
never heard what he'd said to her after they'd
made love. She'd just taken it as a friend helping out another friend. Scratching an itch.

He balled the note up and threw it onto the
floor. She'd gone home, satisfied and satiated.
Feeling happy. And he felt like he'd almost
ripped his heart out of his chest and shown it
to her. If she'd been awake, she'd have heard
it. Him spilling his guts, for nothing. The
minute she'd told him she fancied him, all
sense had gone out of his mind. It was back
now with a vengeance.

It was the 'mate' that did it.

*Cheers, mate. Thanks for the mind-blow-
ing sex, pal.*

Not a sign of anything significant. He'd
taken her home, shown her a good time, just
like he always did. Of course she thought it
meant nothing to him.

He'd shown her time and time again what
he thought of relationships, of being attached
to another person. Hell, she didn't even want
to live with him as a housemate. She'd told
him as much. He was his father's son, all
right. He'd gone and done exactly what he
always did. Messed things up by getting too

involved. It was why he never bothered with relationships. At first, with his past hanging over him, he hadn't wanted to ruin another's life. Then he'd learned to live without them.

He had sex when he needed it. Easy, superficial. No harm done. Not this time. This time he'd done it with his best friend, the one person he loved and respected other than his mother. He'd blown it. He couldn't go back to how it was before now that he'd had a taste of her, but she wasn't his to have. She was only a friend. A *mate*. He thought of everyone at work—if they found out what had happened between them. What they'd think of Molly. They already teased her for being friends with him. He felt his fists clench. He didn't want her tarnished like that. Not his Mol.

He couldn't let them know. He'd just have to forget it. Protect Molly's reputation, and their friendship. If that was all they had left, then so be it. He looked at the rumpled sheets on the bed. The only evidence that last night had happened. He went to rip them off when the phone rang in his trousers.

He scrambled for it despite himself.

'Molly?' He didn't even look at the screen before hitting the answer button.

'No, it's me,' Liam laughed. 'You coming to football today? We could use you.'

Matt sighed, chucking his trousers back on the floor. 'Yeah, why not. I've nothing else to do. You back now then?'

'Yeah.' Matt could tell Liam was smiling through the phone. He sounded so happy. Well, he would, just returning from his honeymoon. Matt almost hated him for it. He hoped he wasn't too euphoric at the match. 'It was amazing.'

'Fantastic,' Matt replied a little too sarcastically. 'I'm thrilled for you.'

'Yeah?' Liam's tone changed. 'What's crawled up your behind? Last night's conquest still hanging around, is she?'

'Nothing, no conquest,' he muttered. 'I'll meet you there.'

'Don't you want a lift? What's up with you?'

'Nothing.' He tried to shake off his bad mood. 'I'm good. Pick me up in twenty.'

'Cool. Breakfast first, on me.'

'I'm not hungry.' He wasn't in the mood to hear about how happy Liam was this morning. He was still reeling from the night before.

'Yeah, well I am.' Liam's mood couldn't be dulled, it seemed. 'And you can tell me what's going on with you, before you take someone's head off on the pitch. Be ready. Be in a better mood when I come.'

Liam rang off without waiting for a response. Matt stared at the phone for a moment, and turning, he swiped the lamp off the side table. It smashed on the floor, and he stared at the broken pieces before stomping off to get a shower. He needed to wash the scent of Molly off his body. It would drive him mad otherwise.

The Eureka Café was busy that morning. Liam was looking, nay simpering, at a cute toddler being fed in a high chair at the next table. Matt looked away, concentrating on his full English. He ripped a slice of toast in half and dipped it in his beans before shovelling it down.

'Are you going to eat your food or not?'

Liam turned from the family. 'I'm eating it. I missed you too, by the way. Are you going to tell me what's up?'

Matt shoved another forkful of food into his mouth, grunting back at his friend and colleague.

'I need words, Matthew.' Liam raised a brow. 'You and Molly fallen out?'

Matt's fork dropped to his plate with a clatter. He picked it up, gingerly. 'What makes you say that?'

'You thought I was her when I rang. You

sounded upset, and you've been a grumpy so-and-so all morning. Spill it.'

'I slept with her.'

'Molly?' His loud voice startled half the café. The toddler made a whimpering noise. Liam nodded his apology to the father, and focused his green eyes back on Matt. 'What the hell are you playing at? It's Molly!'

'I know,' Matt growled. He sighed in frustration, shoving his cutlery back down onto his plate. His appetite was gone. 'I didn't plan it. It just…happened.'

'Well.' Liam wasn't going to let it drop. 'No wonder you're in a sulk. What happened? Eh? You run out of random discreet women to sleep with?'

'It's not like that!' Matt said loudly. He saw people looking and lowered his voice. 'We went out last night, the usual drinks. We went to Passion. Some sleazebag hit on her in the bar. I stepped in, she got mad. It went from there.'

Liam furrowed his brow. 'You got jealous.'

Matt nodded, thinking of how angry he'd felt when he'd come back to find her being hit on. Pure green-tinted rage. 'She told me she liked me. Liam, she liked me that first day. The first day we met. But she never said anything.'

Liam digested that piece of information. They'd spoken about that day before, many times.

'It went from there. I didn't mean for it to happen.' Matt bit his lip. 'Not like this.'

His mate was quiet, taking it in. 'She liked you too? When you first met, the thing with the box?'

Matt nodded, a stricken look on his face. 'Yeah. She never told me, but she said she did. What was I supposed to do? Just say thanks and let her go home? She stayed over at mine, but when I woke up this morning, she was just...gone.'

Liam scooped another bite into his mouth, taking what seemed like an age to chew.

'Now you eat? Tell me what to do!'

Liam swallowed. 'Well, why did she leave? Have you called her?'

'Of course I've called her. Her phone's switched off.' He scraped the rest of the food off his plate, eating it for something to do. His stomach was in knots, and he felt wildly out of control. Like he was pushed so far out of his comfort zone he was on another continent. Without Molly, what would he do? 'She left because she didn't want an awkward morning, probably. She left a note.'

'Saying what?'

Matt swallowed. 'Thanks for the good night. See you soon, mate.' Liam's face said it all. 'I know, I know. You don't have to say it. I messed up.'

Liam threw some bills down on the table, draining his coffee-cup. 'I will anyway, ma pal. You need to think seriously about this. Right now, it's just one night.'

'You weren't there,' Matt protested. 'It wasn't a hookup, Liam. You know how much I care about her.'

'I know it wasn't. It's Molly. She is the best thing in your life. That's why I'm worried. Do you realise what will happen if you screw this up? Everyone at work will hate you.'

'They hate me now.'

'They tolerate you because of Molly. Without her, that's it. It will be impossible to work with her. I don't want that—do you?'

Matt shook his head, his eyes focusing on the tiled floor. 'I like her, Liam. You know that.' When he looked back at his friend, he had to blink to keep the tear that was threatening to escape. Liam brushed his dark brown hair away from his face, the new wedding ring glinting on his finger. Matt couldn't look at it for long. 'I just don't think she feels the same way about me. I'd made peace with it. You know what she wants.'

Liam's lips pursed. 'She wants the whole life. Marriage, kids...'

'Exactly. What do I do?' He pinched the top of his nose between his fingers. 'After last night... I don't know how to go back to just being her friend. I'm not sure I even want to. Do I try this with Molly?'

Matt watched his friend's expression slowly change, and he steeled himself for some hard truths. He knew he had a lot to change, a lot to prove.

'I think you should let it go.'

'What?'

Liam nodded once at him, steepling his fingers with his elbows on the table.

'Let her go. You said it yourself—she thinks it was just a friendship thing. A one-off. Can you really offer Molly what she wants? It's no secret that she wants the whole white picket fence and you don't. I can't see how this won't end in tears. You have a reputation at work already for being aloof, and Molly is the one thing that redeems you there.'

'You think that little of me?' Matt countered. 'Really? Am I that bad?'

Liam sighed heavily. 'No, you're not. Come on. You know I get it, but you and Molly... you're just on different paths. Of course you're not like your dad, but you have to be honest. It's left you more than gun-shy when it comes to commitment. I know your story. So does Molly, but it doesn't change the fact that you want different things from life. Your dad leaving like that, living in his shadow…'

'This isn't about him,' Matt growled. 'I would never hurt Molly like that.'

'I know that, but this *is* about him. Your dad cheated with other women behind your mum's back. He left you both with no money, about to lose the house while he swanned off to his other family with wads of secret cash in his pockets. I don't think you're like him at all.'

'Get to the point, Liam. Tell me why I'm not good enough for Molly.'

'Fine,' Liam sighed. 'You've spent so much time keeping people at bay, you don't know how to let people in. You've spent so much time not being your father, looking after your mother, that you've forgotten to ask yourself what you want in life. Molly is the closest thing to a heart you have. If you mess that up, I just don't know how you'll turn out. She thinks it was a one-off. A friend helping a friend. If I were you, I'd leave it that way. For all your sakes. If you lose Molly, mate, I just don't see it ending well. You need her in your life.' His features softened when he focused on his friend. 'I think you and Molly are great together. We've talked enough about it. I just didn't see it happening. All I'm saying is, if you decide to go with this, with her—you need to be sure it's what you really want or you could do a lot of damage.'

Matt stood up from the table first, putting his napkin down, and then headed for the door. He was almost at Liam's car when his friend caught him up.

'Matt, you know what I'm saying makes sense.' The car beeped as Liam unlocked it. 'I know you're a good man. You took care of your mother, worked your tail off to get where you are. Despite your dad. You love Molly to bits, and she's good for you. Hell, she's the only thing apart from work that makes you human. Having her makes you happy. Are you really going to risk losing that? Can you honestly say you could give her what she wants? What she deserves? Is it even what you want?'

'I don't know,' he muttered. 'It happened last night, Liam. Her side of the bed is still warm. I haven't had a chance to think. I got up, and she'd gone, leaving me a Dear Mate letter.'

'Exactly,' Liam reminded. 'She gave you an out, Matt. All I'm saying is think about it. She's ready, but I don't think you are. You haven't even got over me getting married! Can you honestly say that you'd ever make that commitment, down the line?'

Matt wanted to scream at his friend. Trust Liam to bring him back down to Earth with a well-meaning pep talk. Even if it was true, it was still a bitter pill to swallow.

He could try. God knows he wanted to, but Liam's words were already seeping into his psyche. He knew what Molly deserved. He'd chased off enough reprobates over the years to know what she didn't too. Men like him.

George and Matt's other friends and colleagues all loved Molly, felt protective of her. Almost as much as he did. He wasn't Mr White Picket Fence. He'd seen behind the veil growing up. Those fences held lies, and secrets. His mother had been a broken shell afterwards. People stared at them, whispered at the school gates. He'd decided a long time ago that wasn't the life for him. Any children bearing his name would no doubt bear scrutiny. Could he honestly have a son, and see him go through that?

Could he even be the man Molly wanted? If not, how long would it be till she realised he wasn't? If it went wrong, he didn't want to think about what his life would look like.

She was the only woman he'd ever considered having in his life permanently. If he lost her, he would lose everything. But that was only if he could convince her to give him a shot in the first place.

'I don't know, Liam. I just don't know.' He huffed out a breath. 'I can't lose her.'

Liam walked to the driver-side and opened the door, motioning for his friend to get in. 'I know. I get it. You need Molly, and right now, you can pull this back. I just don't want you to be alone, that's all. We're going to be late to the game.'

They sat in silence for the rest of the journey. Twenty minutes into the match, Matt was red-carded for an aggressive tackle, and stormed off to the changing room to cool off. It didn't work, so after Liam drove him home, he shut the blinds and ignored the world. When he called Molly again, she still didn't pick up. He was losing her already. He could feel it. He'd got closer to her than he'd ever hoped, but it had come at a cost. The house wasn't right without her now. After one night, she'd shattered his bachelor pad's status. And that's when he had the idea. A way to stay close, and not lose her. It wasn't perfect, but Matt already knew when it came to Molly, he would take what he could get.

CHAPTER SEVEN

MOLLY'S TOE SLAMMED painfully into a pile of boxes right by her bedroom door.

'Amy, damn it! Can you move your stuff?' She flounced into the kitchen and flicked the coffee maker on. 'That's the third time this week I've nearly taken myself out.'

'Sorry!' Amy shouted from her bedroom. A second later her hairdryer turned off, and she padded through wearing her old ratty dressing gown.

Molly scowled at it. 'I hope that's not making the move. It's seen better days. You look grubby.'

Amy ignored her, reaching for the teabags in the cupboard. 'I see the cat has its claws out again.'

'Yeah,' Molly retorted. 'And she's liable to scratch you without her coffee.'

Amy took her cup of tea over to the island and went to sit on the stool next to Molly. 'Are

you going to tell me what's up with you?'
She looked rueful. 'Listen, if it's because of
this—' she waved her hand around the flat
'—I told you I could pay rent for a bit, till
you get sorted. I don't want to leave you in
the lurch.'

Molly felt Amy's hand over hers and cracked.
'Don't be daft—you need that money. Sorry. I
know I've been a little grumpy. I'm just tired.
It's not about the flat. Really.'

'Have you not got anywhere sorted yet?'

Molly shook her head. 'Everything's either
too expensive or too much of a rathole to consider. No one's in the market for a roommate.'

'What about Matt?' Amy asked.

'What about him?' She'd barely seen him
in the last two weeks. She'd been picking up
extra shifts, but only when he wasn't on the
rota. She needed the money, and the distrac-
tion.

'He offered to let you move in, didn't he?
It makes sense to me. He's got a big place,
plenty of room.'

'So?'

'Wow, Molly.' Amy threw her an indignant
look. 'Can you stop biting my head off? I just
want you to be settled, that's all. I feel so bad
leaving you like this. Like, it's my fault. I told
Anton we could wait a bit longer for the wed-

ding, but I practically live at his place as it is, with all the shifts we've been doing.'

Molly sighed, 'Amy, I don't blame you. How could I? I'm so happy for you both, really. I've just been working a lot lately. It's not your fault, I promise.' She hugged her friend to her. 'Ugh, have you bought a new perfume?' She scrunched her nose up against the smell.

Amy swiped at her playfully as they pulled away from each other. 'Hey! No, I always wear this.' Molly frowned. 'You love it normally. Don't you remember, we got it from that little place in Brighton?'

She took another sniff, but her stomach roiled.

Weird.

'Sorry, I feel a bit off lately. Overtired maybe.' She pulled away from the smell, willing her stomach to stop churning.

'And stressed,' Amy said pointedly. 'This is not just about work. I've not seen Matt around here lately. Is he avoiding your moody face too?'

Molly couldn't look Amy in the eye. 'Something like that.' She held her breath to hug her friend. 'I'm going to get dressed.' She plastered on a smile. 'I am happy for you, Amy. I really am.'

Her friend hugged her tight. 'Thank you. I know it will come right for you, Molly. You deserve it.'

Molly nodded, heading to her room.

I do deserve it, she thought to herself as she dressed for work.

The thing was, she'd learned early on that not everyone got their happy-ever-after, no matter how hard they wished for it.

Molly was still thinking about what Amy had said that morning whenever she had a spare moment at work. She'd never answered her about Matt, just dismissed it as them both being busy. Hardly a lie. She'd lived and breathed work since the night they'd spent together, and judging from the rota, so had he. She noticed that even though Liam was back at work, Matt was still picking up extra shifts, mostly on the night shifts that she never worked.

Is he avoiding me too?

'How are things coming along?' she said cheerily as she entered delivery suite four. They were all named after trees, this one being the Sycamore Suite. Liz Masters was sitting on a birthing ball, bouncing away and puffing out steady breaths.

'Not bad, but she's been complaining of a fair bit of pain though.' Billy, her partner, was squatting next to her, a cup of water in his hand, which Liz kept trying to swat away.

'Fair bit of pain? Fair bit? I feel like I'm being squeezed in a vice down there.' Molly and Billy helped her back over to the bed to be examined properly.

After washing her hands and donning a pair of gloves, Molly checked the dilation of Liz's cervix and winced. 'Sorry, guys, we're still only at four centimetres. It might be a while before the little one starts to show.'

Liz groaned, and Billy offered her the water again. 'Billy, I don't want a drink of water. Will you buzz off already?'

'Darling,' he soothed, trying to placate his very pregnant and irritated girlfriend. 'Please, you need to keep your fluids up. The book says—'

Another contraction started to take hold, and Liz snarled something about shoving the book somewhere unpleasant, before the pain started to grip. Molly passed her the gas and air, and she sucked on it till the pain subsided. Molly put the Doppler wand onto her stomach and was satisfied when she heard the baby's strong heartbeat. Everything was on track for their first baby to arrive and make this couple a family.

'Better?' Billy tenderly stroked Liz's hair, leaning in to give her a kiss.

She kissed him back, starting to sob a little. 'Sorry. I can't help it. I'm scared. What if we can't do this?'

Molly kept herself busy, updating the charts, checking everything was in order, but she listened in. It was hard not to.

Billy shushed his girlfriend immediately. 'You're doing great. I told you; we got this, baby.'

'I know, but we don't even live together. We don't have a schedule.'

'So?' Billy laughed, taking Liz's hands in his and sitting down on the bed next to her. 'None of this was on schedule. We'd been on five dates; I didn't even meet your friends! You didn't know my middle name was Eugene.' Liz laughed through her tears, and Billy's whole face lit up. The way he was looking at her reminded Molly of Matt. She had to look away.

'Exactly,' Liz said, her laughter dissolving into fear once more. 'A baby isn't easy. I've got work, and you're trying to make partner at the firm… It's…impossible.'

'Nothing is impossible,' Billy refuted, taking her face between his hands and kissing her forehead. 'I know I love you, Liz, and our baby. Sure, it's fast, but we're not exactly strangers. I fancied you at work for so long, I still can't believe you looked twice at me.'

Molly should have left the room, but when he'd started speaking, she couldn't stop listening. The pair of them didn't even notice that she was there any more. They only had eyes for each other.

'Don't be daft.' Liz was laughing again. 'I liked you too. I just thought we'd have a bit more time together as a couple, you know?' She rubbed her bump affectionately, and Billy leaned down to kiss it.

'I don't regret a thing, baby. Sure, it's going to be hard, but we'll make it work. You and me, remember? That's all we need.'

Molly left the room then, slipping out of the door before she intruded on their moment any further. The next contraction would hit soon, but Liz was going to be a while yet before she delivered. She turned to check on the next patient and barrelled straight into a wall of muscle.

Hands closed tight around her. She bounced right back off the person and was heading to the floor when they caught her. 'Sorry, Doctor!' She'd pushed out a rushed apology to the flash of white coat before realising who it was. Matt's eyes locked on to hers.

'Are you okay?' He searched her face, and she found herself looking away.

She was far too close to him. It was sending her body into overdrive. Aftershocks of their night together were flaming up her face. She was worried this might happen. Her body seemed to refuse to forget his touch. *Traitor*, she chided herself, trying to act normal when she felt anything but. *I was sure he wasn't on shift.*

'Yeah, of course!' She trilled, making the mistake of putting her hands on his chest to put some distance between them. She could feel the warmth of him through his scrub top. Pulling her hands away as though she'd been burned, she tried to recover herself. 'Thanks for…you know, catching me.'

'Always,' he muttered. 'You've not been around lately.'

'Are you kidding?' She tried to laugh but it fell flat. 'I've practically lived here.' *You have too*, she wanted to add, but then he'd know she'd been stalking his rota like a lovesick groupie. Not very well either, since she hadn't foreseen this happening.

'I don't mean at work.' The blue of his eyes looked duller today. Like a watered-down version of their usual brilliance. The dark circles under his eyes were hard to miss too. Even his hair was mussed up. 'Are you…' He looked up and down the corridor. 'Are you avoiding me?' His voice was low, a pleading tone running through it. 'I know that we—'

'Matt, come on. I know the score.'

'Really.' His brows were furrowed, deep. 'You know, huh?' He took a step back from her, cleared his throat.

Over his shoulder she could see George walking down the corridor towards them, pushing a patient in a wheelchair. 'Yes, of course. We're fine,' she said breezily. 'Listen, I need to get on. Catch you later, okay?' She went to leave but felt Matt's fingers brush against hers.

'I miss you, Molly. I don't like how we've been lately. We're both on the same shift today, so I'll take you home afterwards. We can go for some food.'

Did he plan this?

She looked for telltale signs, but he seemed like he did any other day.

Stop being paranoid. He takes you home all the time.

'Wait for me in our usual spot, okay?'

Before she could answer, he was heading down the corridor. Liz's call button went off, and the moment to get out of Matt's offer was gone. *I miss you too*, she thought. Looking at his retreating back, how straight and tense he was, she knew he'd changed. He was less relaxed, less the happy-go-lucky Matt she was used to. She should never have told him she fancied him, or let him think of her that way. They'd crossed the line, and now he felt awkward and she felt gutted. Gutted that they had to go back to the friendship she loved, knowing that was all it was. All it was ever going to be again. He'd already moved on. He hadn't changed his pattern; she'd just become woven into the fabric.

When she'd woken up that Sunday morning in his arms, she'd panicked. He was still coiled around her, and she'd loved it. Too much. She wanted to wake him up and do it all over again. Several times. She wanted to go to his football match with him, cheer him on from the sidelines like she always did.

The knowledge of how that muscular body had made her come so hard just hours earlier had been roiling inside her. She'd never experienced anything like that before. She wasn't some virgin, but she knew that no other man had come remotely close to giving her the pleasure he had that night. She doubted that anyone would again, and that thought depressed the hell out of her. She needed to feel it again, feel him.

'Everything okay?' she said jovially as she entered the birthing suite. A second later, she was dashing across the room and hitting the emergency button on the back of the wall.

Billy was shouting, panic evident in his voice. 'What's wrong with her? She was fine, and then she couldn't breathe!'

Liz was pale, gasping for breath. Clutching at her stomach. Lifting the sheet covering her legs, Molly saw the unmistakable sign of blood.

'It's the pain. It hurts so much! Something's wrong!'

The doors to the delivery suite banged open, and there was Matt, George and Ella, one of the other midwives. Ella ran over to Billy, telling him everything was okay, that they were there to help. She ushered him out of the room, telling him his family was in the best place. The atmosphere in the room intensified the second they were outside the suite.

'Elizabeth Masters, twenty-eight. Suspected placental abruption. First child. No health issues. Patient is forty plus four, normal pregnancy, no issues.'

Liz was screaming in pain, asking over and over what was wrong with her baby as Molly fired off her patient information. Matt moved into action the second he got the update.

'I'm Dr Loren, Liz. We need to get you into theatre. Your placenta has detached, and it's causing the baby some distress. We need to move fast to get the baby delivered safely, and I need you to trust me. Okay?' Molly and George were already prepping her to move, throwing the bed sides up, putting a monitor on the baby. The fetus was doing well so far, but that would soon change. Liz started to nod, a panicked look on her face. Matt took her hand. 'We've got you,' he said confidently, before flicking his gaze to Molly. 'Let's move.'

The second they hit the operating room, it was all systems go. Matt was gowned and gloved, Liz was given sedation and Ella was comforting Billy in the family room. They could hear him crying as they ran past with Liz on the gurney.

'She's lost a lot of blood. Hang O neg now. Let's get her ready to be transfused. Call the blood bank.' Matt checked the field was ready, iodine tinging the flesh of Liz's extended stomach. 'Scalpel.'

He got to work, no time for screens, as there was no need. Molly sat on the monitor, checking the baby's vitals.

'Status,' he barked at her in his usual shorthand.

'Heart rate is starting to deteriorate. Move fast.'

Matt nodded once, his hands moving effortlessly to perform the Caesarean. After what felt like only several long minutes later, he was lifting the baby free, into the waiting arms of George. The midwife wrapped the baby in a towel, taking it over to the other side of the room. Molly ran to help, and they suctioned the nose and mouth, rubbing the blood and mucus off the baby and checking her over. They were rewarded seconds later with a very healthy and lusty cry from the newborn girl.

'Fantastic. All good?' Matt called over, working on Liz. 'Mum is stable, but we need to monitor her. She lost a lot of blood. Transfusing well.'

Molly was clamping the placenta and cutting the spongy cord that connected mother to child, checking it was intact. 'Baby girl, all good,' she reported. 'Vitals are good. No need for oxygen.'

'Nice colour too.' George smiled, running a gloved finger along one of her little fists.

'Excellent,' Matt replied. 'George, can you let the father know please? He'll be worried.'

George raised a surprised brow. 'Er, yeah. Sure. Of course. Molly, you got her?' He nodded towards the baby, and Molly smiled back.

'Of course. You go.'

George gave a nod to Matt, something he didn't usually do.

'Careful,' Molly said when they were alone with mother and baby. Matt was just closing Liz's operation site up; the nurses would already be en route to wheel her through to recovery. She'd be awake soon, and no doubt eager to meet her child. 'George might think you have a heart if you show your humanity like that.' She was teasing, but as he pulled off his mask, she could see that he didn't like the comment. 'Matt, I was only joking.'

Two of the nurses came in and took Liz and the baby away, leaving Matt and Molly in the room. It suddenly felt so large, and the distance between them so far.

'I know,' he said, shrugging. 'Figured I could try harder to be a bit nicer, that's all. See you tonight.' He was gone with a swish of the doors before she could even open her mouth to stop him. Not for the first time that day, she felt sick to her stomach. The can of worms was wriggling, making its presence known again.

The rest of the shift passed without event. Liz was sore, shell-shocked but recovering well. Billy had done nothing but cry and kiss her since the second they were reunited. It seemed that all their previous fears were forgotten. They were just thrilled to be a family. They'd already faced a nightmare, and now their little girl was here. They'd called her Isabella, and the pair of them couldn't stop looking at each other.

Molly was still high from being around them when she got into Matt's waiting car. 'Hi,' she said, leaning in to drop a kiss on his cheek like she always did. His brows raised, his head half turning towards her.

'Hi.' He smiled. 'Liz is doing well. I checked in on them before I left.'

'I know. they're such a cute couple. They met at work you know. I think it was a bit of a surprise, whirlwind romance.' Matt was pulling out of the car park, and she noticed he'd turned in the direction of his house. 'We not eating out?'

'Not tonight.' He looked distracted. 'They met at work?'

'Yeah.' Molly nodded, grateful that the tension from before seemed to be easing. It was still a bit awkward, but that was understandable. They'd seen each other naked, after all. Worshipped each other's bodies. It was bound to be odd for a while. She could get a handle on it. The next time he was with one of his hookups was what she was dreading. It would happen eventually. She knew that would make it easier to forget what they'd done together though. Make it less special. Allow her to see it for what it was, once and for all. A one-off. A mistake. 'I love the two of them together.'

Matt said nothing. Molly waited, but after two turns of silence, she pressed the radio on. Anything to fill the space between them.

'You got anywhere to live yet?' His eyes were firmly on the road.

'No,' she sighed. 'Nothing. I rang another letting agency at lunch, but everything in my price range already has a waiting list.' She pulled a face. 'Amy's offered to pay the rent a bit longer, but I can't let her do that.'

'The offer's still there, to move in with me.'

She was saved from answering by his

phone. He clicked the answer button just as he pulled onto his drive.

He took me to his house.

'Hi, Mum, you okay? You're on speakerphone.'

'Hello, darling. I just wanted to check you got the wedding invitation.'

He looked across at Molly, seizing his lip between his teeth. 'Yeah, I got it. You didn't need to send me one though, surely? I am walking you down the aisle.'

'I know. Is Molly with you?'

Matt blushed. Molly spotted it a mile off.

'Yes, Sarah, I'm here. I didn't get an invitation! What's up with that?'

Sarah laughed. 'Yes, you did. I put you on Matt's.' She paused. 'Didn't he tell you?'

Matt was firmly eyes front, as though he wanted the conversation to be over.

'Oh, we've both been busy working lately. I can't wait until your big day, thank you.'

'Well, as long as you're both there, that's all I care about. Have you decided whether you're going to move in with Matt yet?'

Oh, God, he'd told his mother. What else had he told her?

She felt her cheeks redden. 'Er…well…'

Matt cut in. 'Yes, actually. We're just talking about the logistics of it.'

'Matt—' Molly started. 'We—'

'Mum, I'm sorry. Can I call you back? We just pulled up.'

'Yes, love, of course. Night, Molly!'

The second the call ended; Matt turned to her. 'Look, I know it's been weird between us. We've both been avoiding each other.'

'No, I haven't.'

'Yes, you have.' He fixed her with his stern stare. It silenced her. 'I have too. It's been weird.'

Weird is an understatement. How the hell am I going to set foot in his house again tonight, let alone live there? Not. A. Chance.

'Listen, we're friends. Best friends. That can never, ever change. I want you to live with me. You need somewhere to live. What's the point in looking for a housemate or another flat? You know me better than anyone.'

'True, but…'

'Molly, I'm tired of this. It's not charity. You'd pay rent, get your own food. I have the space, and I could use the company. I don't want you to live with some stranger. You know as well as I do that you like your space. Just say yes and do us both a favour.' There it was again. That bleak expression. 'I know you need to feel safe in your own home.' He levelled her with a look so sure, she wanted to take him into her arms. She didn't. 'I make you feel safe. Right?'

'Right. Always,' she acknowledged. 'I do feel safe with you.'

His triumphant grin said it all. 'Good. That's that then. We'll go get your things on our next day off. Come on.' He jerked his head towards his house. 'Let's go home. I'm ordering extra spring rolls tonight from your favourite place. I feel like celebrating.'

Molly grinned back in relief before pulling him in for a hug. Finally, this was her Matt, happy again. Taking care of her in his own special little way. Their friendship was back. Perhaps living with him wouldn't be so bad after all. He was so set on it. Perhaps the other night was already fading into their past. She didn't know whether to be sad or happy, but this way, she at least had Matt in her life.

'Just for a little while,' she relented. 'Till I get sorted.'

Matt's smile was dazzling. 'As long as you need.' He gave her a squeeze, and she sank into his arms. 'No rush,' he muttered into her hair. 'Welcome home, roomie.'

CHAPTER EIGHT

IT WAS CLINIC DAY, and Molly was on shift with Matt. He had a full roster of patients, and the schedule was so full she hadn't stopped all morning. Which would be great, except the pancakes he'd made them that morning were lying heavy in her stomach. She'd been living with Matt a little over three weeks. For the most part, it had been fine.

Awkward at first. She remembered the first night. Going to bed at the same time. Him saying goodnight to her on the stairs, then leaning down to kiss her. She'd turned in panic at the last minute, wondering if he was going for the lips, half hoping, half dreading that he was. She couldn't survive another night of the Loren experience. She'd catch more feelings than butterflies with a net, and they were already flying around in the pit of her stomach. He'd simply pecked her cheek.

Today she felt like something was wiggling

around inside her, but it felt more like worms this time. She got to the cafeteria, and George waved her over.

'Hey, come sit with me.' He was tucking into avocado on toast, and Molly wrinkled her nose up at it.

'Er, just let me get some coffee first.'

George indicated his full mug. 'Take mine. I have a juice as well.'

Molly took a seat next to him. She raised the cup to her lips, but the smell repelled her. 'Yuck.' She pushed it away from her. 'I think the milk's off.'

'Don't drink it then. How's clinic going? The labour ward is steady, not many in so far. No planned C-sections.'

They worked it that way the best they could alongside the clinic days, freeing up at least one doctor per day to work with the patients, monitor their pregnancies.

'Good. Rammed though. This is the first chance I've had to breathe all day.'

George offered her one of his slices of buttered toast. She waved it away.

'Not hungry?' he asked.

'Nope. I feel a bit sick. Matt made pancakes.'

George's eyebrows hit the ceiling. 'Really? Was he half-naked when he did it?' Typical

George. He might not be Matt's biggest fan, but he could appreciate a good-looking man when he saw one.

'What? No.' Molly blushed at the thought. Matt had only been wearing a robe and boxer shorts, come to think of it. The robe was open too, hence the reason she knew he wore black silky-looking boxers. The night they'd spent together he'd slept naked. They both had. She snapped the image of Matt and his naked body out of her head.

'I told you—it's only temporary. Us living together, I mean.' She pushed George's coffee-cup further away with her hand. She could still smell it. 'I'm going back to work. See you.'

She headed back to the clinic area, checking everything was good at the nurses' station. Saying hello to a couple of colleagues as she passed them. She noticed a few odd glances, but given she was feeling a bit ropy, she knew her face probably looked a little pale. But it was more than that.

Her stomach was really off. With the move, she'd been burning the candle at both ends. She felt so out of sorts lately. Different. She just wanted to get the day over with. Get home and sink her tired, aching body into a bubble bath. She had a sudden image of Matt covered in suds, and blinked it away.

At reception, she picked up the next three patient records from the basket. Pasting on her best grin for the people sat on chairs in the waiting-room, she focused on the tasks ahead.

'Miss Pinkman?'

CHAPTER NINE

'WELL, MISS PINKMAN.' Matt smiled. 'Everything looks perfectly healthy.' He looked away from the file of charts and scans in front of him, steepling his fingers, elbows on his desk. 'I see no reason why we can't proceed as arranged.'

'Oh, thank God.' The relief on Ellie Pinkman's face was palpable. 'I can't wait to tell Eric. It's been so scary.'

'I know,' Matt said earnestly. 'Third trimester now, and everything looks great. Keep doing what you are doing, and your baby will be here before you know it.'

He reached over to the other side of his desk to select a pamphlet from a stack he kept. 'I know we've discussed this before, but I do think that speaking to someone about what you've been through would be beneficial. When you're ready, of course. We're here to support you.'

He pushed the pamphlet for the miscarriage support group across the table, just as Molly came back into the room. She'd been called out to assist with a birth, and Matt's whole body vibrated when she entered.

It had been so hard living with her. Seeing her every morning, every night. A kind of beautiful torture he couldn't get enough of or give up. He knew she'd been looking for somewhere else to live still. He'd seen the circled newspaper listings she'd left on the coffee table. She'd shoved them out of the way whenever he entered the room, but he wasn't stupid.

He had been thinking about how to get her to stay with him ever since. Liam thought he was daft, 'asking for trouble' as he'd put it. One night, when Matt had come home to Molly doing yoga in the front room in tight-fitting pink yoga pants that Matt wanted to rip off with his bare teeth, he'd barely got out of there alive. He'd called Liam, begging him to leave his new wife for the night and come out and have a drink with him. He'd had so many cold showers, he didn't know how he had any skin left. Even Molly had commented on the amount of empty shower gel bottles in the recycling bin. He'd changed to soap to throw her off the scent, no pun intended.

He realised that he'd spaced out at the worst possible time and scowled at himself. Molly caught his look, her face falling, and he flushed.

Damn it, now she thinks I'm mad at her again. I can't help it; I'm mad at the situation. So mad. I'm in a prison of my own making.

'You really think I need a support group?' Miss Pinkman asked. 'Everything's fine now.'

Matt nodded, smiling. 'Everything is great. Your baby is healthy and on track for a textbook delivery.' He patted the file. 'We've been extra cautious with your care. But given what you've been through…'

'The miscarriages,' she supplied glumly. She looked down at the pamphlet again and tucked it into her handbag. 'I'll call them. I know you're right, doctor. My family have been saying the same.' She sighed heavily.

Behind him, Molly was listening but looking through the patient records. Discreet and caring as always. She looked a little pale under the harsh strip lighting of the room. Come to think of it, she'd been a bit off in general lately. Perhaps she was feeling awkward about their living arrangements too, just without the cold showers and the dirty dreams.

'Thank you, Dr Loren. I mean it—you've really been there for us both through all this.'

'No problem,' he said gently. 'Happy to help. Let's see you again in a week, ten days. Okay?' He signed the appointment request form, filling in the timescale, and passed it to her with a flourish of his wrist. 'Remember, plenty of rest and hydrate.'

Miss Pinkman nodded with a happy, watery smile. She squeezed Molly's shoulder as she left. 'Thank you. Both.'

Molly picked up the next file from the pile and deposited it onto his desk.

'Ready for the next one?'

'In a minute. I have lunch coming. I got one of the nurses to bring it up, cut down the time a bit.' He sighed, rubbing his hands down his face. He could feel the day-old stubble. For a man who spent so much time in the shower, he really needed to up his shaving regime. 'Can you ask the next patient to wait a few minutes?' Molly nodded, looking like she wanted to say something. She was rubbish; she could never hide her feelings. They were always displayed on her face. He just wished he could read how she really felt about him. 'Tell me what's up.'

There was a knock at the door, and she held up a finger. 'Thanks, Josie,' she said to

the woman outside, taking a package of sandwiches and drinks from her.

'Cheers. Can you tell reception the doctor
is on a break please? I'll come for the next
patient when he's ready.'

'No problem. I put some in for you too. Just
ham and cheese.'

Molly didn't look happy about that, and
Matt wondered what was going on. He took
the package from her and spread it out on the
table. He had hot beef and mustard, one of his
favourite sandwiches from the new menu. He
noticed that Molly had sat down at the other
side of the desk but was sipping gingerly at
one of the orange juices.

'You already ate?' He opened the brown
paper bag and was about to take a bite of his
sandwich when Molly turned green. 'Mol,
what's wrong?'

'The mustard.' She managed to get the
words out before gagging. 'It stinks.'

Matt's brow rose. 'What? You love mustard.' He sniffed at his lunch, and Molly
heaved. She ran to the waste-paper basket in
the corner and threw up violently. Matt hur-
ried to her side.

'That's it, get it out,' he soothed, pulling
a blond strand of hair back behind her ear.

'Hell. Are you okay?' He rubbed her back, his hand moving in slow circles as she retched.

'No,' she said finally, standing up slowly and reaching for a paper towel from the dispenser. 'I think you poisoned me with your pancakes.'

He grabbed her orange juice. 'Here, drink this. My pancakes are perfect too, cheeky.' His hand was on her cheek before he thought twice about it. 'Seriously, are you okay? You look awful.'

'Thanks,' she muttered, pushing his hand off when he checked her forehead temperature. 'Love you too.' She went to leave, but he closed his hand around hers.

'Steady. Come and sit down. You can clean up in a minute.' He pulled her over to the chair, and she came with him willingly. He could see that she was shaking. 'Have you not eaten since breakfast?'

She shook her head, reaching over to the bowl he kept on his table and popping a mint imperial into her mouth. She sucked on it, and her colour returned. Just a little. He still didn't like the look of her though. 'I couldn't stomach it. I think I might have a bug.'

'Right.' Matt pointed to the juice in her hand. 'Drink that.' She glowered at him. 'Please.'

She rolled her eyes, but slowly sipped at it till it was empty. He was watching her, and something else clicked in his brain. 'What other symptoms do you have, other than the sense of smell being off, and the nausea.'

She thought for a moment. 'Nothing much. I've felt a bit tired, maybe. Nothing major. Why?'

Matt couldn't answer her. It was all clicking together in his mind, and he felt sick himself.

It couldn't be, could it?

This time he was the one shaking. He picked up the phone on his desk, then called through to reception.

'Jane? Yeah, listen. I've had an emergency come up. Can you rearrange the clinic and let Liam know? Yes. No, I don't think I'll be back in for the afternoon. Nurse Molly is coming with me too.' Molly was looking at him as if he'd gone mad. He grabbed his bag, flicking his answering machine on. 'Come on,' he commanded, standing before her and reaching out his hand. 'Let's go.'

'Matt, what the hell? We can't just leave work.'

'It's a one-off, and you're sick. You can't work like this.'

'So?' She shook her head. 'I'll be fine.'

'Molly, move your backside. We're going home, now. Either you walk out of here, or I'll carry you out.'

Her look was incredulous, but Matt ignored her. He needed to get her out of here. He needed to know. God, he needed to know right now. He wasn't going to be able to concentrate anyway. Molly looked so pale, he wanted to get her home. Look after her.

'Matt, you're being weird. It's just a bug. I'm fine. This overprotective side of you gets right on my wick.'

'Yeah?' he said, grabbing her bag from where she kept it under the counter and passing it to her. 'Well, get used to it,' he half growled. She huffed but got to her feet. They walked out together, and he was driving towards his house in minutes. When they reached the parade of shops near his place, he parked and rushed into the chemist, leaving Molly in the car looking bewildered.

'You think I'm pregnant?' Molly was laughing, but he didn't laugh back. Molly stared at him aghast, but she could almost feel the cogs turning in her brain. Clicking into place with a resounding thud. 'I'm not pregnant.' There was a lot less conviction in her voice the second time around.

They were standing in his kitchen, the contents of the bag from the chemist spilled out on the counter. Pregnancy tests, Pepto, bottles of water.

'Molly, put it together. Think of your symptoms. You love coffee and mustard on everything, but you've gone off them both. You threw up. You feel tired.'

'Oh, God…' She sagged against the counter, picking up one of the tests with a glazed expression. 'Oh, no.'

Matt's jaw flexed. 'It's okay.'

'Okay?' she echoed. 'How is this going to be okay?'

She felt his arms come around her, and she went to him. She could feel him kissing the top of her head, his arms encircling her tight.

'Let's just find out, okay? I'm here.'

He walked with her up the stairs, to the main bathroom. She could barely put one foot in front of the other her mind was racing so much. His steps were strong, sure and he kept her upright in his arms. She still had the box in her hands, and she looked down at it again. 'I can't believe I didn't think about it.' She laughed, but it was short-lived, hollow. 'I'm a midwife, and I never twigged. We used protection.'

Matt's face looked stricken, and she

couldn't bear to look at it for long. What a mess. He didn't want this; she was sure of it. He looked as sick as she felt.

'Don't worry about any of that now. Let's just find out and take it from there.'

He went to follow her into the bathroom, but she put her hand on his chest. Stilling him.

'I think I've got it from here.' They both smiled wryly, realising that he was about to watch her pee onto a stick. 'I know we're close, but there's a limit. Even to our friend-ship.'

'Molly, if you are—'

'I won't be,' she lied, even to herself. 'Don't worry.'

'I'm not worried. I...' He nodded to the bathroom. 'I'll go downstairs. Make us a drink. Come find me?'

She nodded, watching him walk down the stairs. He'd held her hand the whole way up, and his fingers were the last to leave her. She waited till she heard him moving around in the kitchen, and then closed the bathroom door behind her.

The fancy mirror in his bathroom was lit up from behind by a bright LED. It made the tinge of her skin look all the greener. 'You are an idiot,' she said to her reflection in the mirror. 'You are a total idiot.'

Once she'd ripped open the box, she looked at the stick. It wasn't like she needed to read the instructions. She'd been dealing with pregnancies for so long; she wasn't exactly a novice. It was the first time she'd had reason to take one though. They'd used a condom, but it didn't surprise her that it might not have worked. They weren't infallible. She'd delivered enough results of them failing to know that, but now it was her. Her and Matt. Hell, there was the nausea again. Things had only just got back to normal with him. Normalish anyway. They were living together, for God's sake. And now a baby?

Being a broke single mum was the opposite of everything she'd strived to become. It was her mother's life, minus the dead beat surrogate dads hanging around. The absent, erratic parenting. And Matt. He wasn't exactly Mr Commitment, was he? He'd probably already had another romantic encounter since their night. Yet he hadn't mentioned anything. She'd seen no signs. Especially not since moving in. She'd half expected to be alone on her nights off, but he was nearly always around, or very occasionally out with Liam.

She knew he never had women in his house, so she was grateful for that rule.

What would he say knowing his bachelor pad might end up needing a nursery? He'd grow to resent her. Hate her even. She'd seen it before, on the faces of a few of the expectant fathers in the delivery rooms. The hookups that had resulted in a baby. Some couples were just not cut out to be parents together. Her own parents for one. Now she was possibly repeating history and dragging Matt along for the ride. She'd never be able to move out if that was the case.

'Mol?' A soft knock at the door. 'I brought you some water, if you need it.'

'No!' she half barked back. 'No, I'm good.' The orange juice was already doing the job. She just couldn't bring herself to take the test. Ear at the door, she heard shuffling movements. 'You still there?'

'Yeah.'

'Are you really going to listen to me pee?'

'I'm going.' She heard him on the stairs. He'd be back soon.

What am I going to do? Hide in the bathroom for ever?

Taking a deep breath, she ripped the wrapper off the test. This was it. One little bodily function would decide the rest of her life. Their lives.

The test sat on the closed toilet lid, resting on a piece of folded-up toilet roll. It was odd. She'd heard about so many other women's moments like these. Happy tears. Sad tears. The angst and excitement, the fear and trepidation they felt while waiting for those three long minutes to pass. To see the liquid soak into the litmus paper, illuminating one line or two. A cross or no cross. A word saying yay, or not today. When the result came up, it took her breath away. Ripped the air right out of her lungs for a moment. She tried to breathe deeper, but her windpipe wouldn't work. She clawed at the door handle, wanting to run down the stairs. To Matt. She needed Matt.

'Molly?' Matt was right there, the wooden door the only thing between them. He'd never left. 'Molly?'

His arms were around her, strong. Steadfast as always. She looked up at him, and the second she locked gazes with him, saw the striking blue of his eyes, she caught her breath. Found her voice.

'We're having a baby,' she said, and passed out in his arms. The last thing she remembered was Matt calling her name, telling her he was there for her. Always.

CHAPTER TEN

MATT PUT HER to sleep in his bed. He'd tell her tomorrow it was because she'd left her bed a mess that morning, clothes strewn across it, and he didn't want to disturb her stuff. Which was true to a certain degree, but the real truth was that he wanted her close to him. She was carrying his child. The shock of it had made her pass out. He'd managed to get some chicken soup and water into her when she came round, but she didn't say anything. She looked so tired, so drawn. He didn't trust himself to talk about it. So they didn't. He took care of her instead. Showed her with actions that he was there. There would be plenty of time for talking later.

Once he was sure she was settled for the night, he'd come back downstairs. Molly would need the day off work, he knew. He could arrange cover for her at the centre. But first, he needed a stiff Scotch. Plan his next move. Digest the news that he was going to be a father. His best friend was having his baby. After one night together. It was the stuff of his clients' stories. The reason why many of them ended up in his office and in the delivery rooms at the Ashford. Fleeting little moments that ended in permanence. That's what they were now, more than ever—permanence personified.

Sighing heavily, he picked up his phone.

'Mum? Yeah, it's me. I'm fine.' It was so good to hear her voice. Whenever he had a problem as a child, he'd always go to his mum over his father. Even before his father wasn't there to call on any more. It was as if he knew at a young age his dad couldn't be relied on.

'No work today?' she asked.

'I was earlier. Something came up.' He could hear her intake of breath. 'Molly's pregnant.'

Wow, saying it out loud makes it real. He couldn't stop the smile that came out. *Molly's having my baby. Wow.*

'She found out today. She's in bed resting. She's tired out.'

He heard his mother's footsteps, and he knew she was heading back up to the house. He could almost pinpoint how many steps she had left before she was back inside his childhood home.

'Is Molly okay?' she asked softly.

'She's shocked, I think.'

'Understandable, my love. Having a baby is an adjustment, no matter how prepared you are. What is she going to do? Is she keeping it?'

Matt's blood ran cold at the thought of Molly not having the baby. She'd always wanted one, but would she want it with him? He'd never considered that scenario.

'I...er... I don't know.' Another conversation that they needed to have when she woke up. He heard his mother pour a drink, the chink of ice as it hit glass.

'Bit early, isn't it?' he quipped, trying to lighten the mood and cancel out some of the dark thoughts swirling around his head. 'Brandy already?' His mother was a sucker for a brandy on the rocks.

'Well,' she retorted, her soft tinkly laugh like a balm to his jagged nerves, 'it's not every day your son tells you he's going to be a father.'

Matt could almost feel his ears bug out of his head. 'How did you know the baby's mine?'

'Oh, give over, I'm not old yet. Of course

it's yours. I didn't realise you'd finally done something about it.'

'Done something about what?'

'About your friendship. God, son, we've all wanted to bang your heads together for the longest time. She's the best thing in your life.'

'Exactly,' he grumbled. 'And now look how that's turned out. I've ruined her life, Mum.'

'Don't be ridiculous! How can you say that? I never thought that when I had you. Never.'

'I don't mean it like that. I mean, I tanked her chances to be with someone she can love, Mum. You know Molly—she deserves better than…this.' He thought he heard a noise from the stairs, and he went quiet, listening. But all was silent.

'Matt,' his mother said firmly. 'You are not your father. What exactly do you think she's looking for that you can't give her?'

'Everything!' he exclaimed. 'Molly wants the whole white picket fence thing. She wants the husband, and the family. She wants a good, normal life. I can't do that. I don't even know how to! Don't you see? This baby…this baby changes everything. It's all…ruined.'

He turned his back, looking out of the window of the house he'd bought years ago. When everyone else was partying or spending money on rent or university functions, he'd stayed home with his mother. Saved every penny. Worked every shift. Stayed up nights learning, studying. To be the doctor, the man he wanted to be. It didn't matter. None of it made a difference. When people heard the name Loren, their eyes narrowed. It had taken years for both him and his mother to come out from under the Loren curse, or the worst of it anyway.

Now his mother wasn't having it, telling him he was nothing like his father. He'd already tuned her out. He always did. She meant well. She loved the bones of him, but she was biased. She didn't know how damaged he was on the inside. He'd always kept it from her. Kept it from everyone.

Almost everyone.

He heard Molly coming down the stairs. 'Mum, Molly just woke up. I have to go. Call you later, okay?'

His mother went to say something else, but he cut the call.

'Hi.' He turned to face her. 'How are you feeling?'

She walked past him, and reached for a glass from the cupboard.

'Better, thanks. Sorry I scared you.'

'Don't be daft. You hungry?'

She nodded but stilled his arm when he started to go to the fridge.

'Let's just get takeout. Listen, I have something to say first. Will you sit?'

He waited till she'd taken a stool to be sure he could sit on the one next to her. He pulled her seat a little closer, and she let him. 'Mol, about—'

'I need to speak first.' She put her finger against his lips. 'I just want you to know that I'm keeping the baby. I want it. Her. Him. Whichever.'

He tried to say *good*, but she pushed her finger harder against his mouth.

'I just thought you should know.' She pulled her finger away. 'I know that this wasn't part of the plan, at all. For either of us. I don't expect anything from you. I just want you to know that too. I don't want to derail your life, any more than I already have.'

'What makes you think I won't want to be involved?' He felt sick. *She's living in my house, carrying my child, and she feels further away than ever.* 'It's my child too. I can help. I want to help. More than help. God, this is not coming out right at all.'

Damn it, I don't want to just help. I want to be a family. I wish I could do that. I wish it was in me. You see it too, don't you?

'We both know that us sleeping together was a mistake.' She was looking at a point over his shoulder now, then the floor. Anywhere but into his eyes. 'We got drunk, and it should never have happened. I was sad and feeling lost. I shouldn't have confused things.' She drew herself up to her full height. 'But I can do this on my own.'

'No,' he said, his fear and disappointment turning into anger. She'd not even considered him as a father. That they could do this together. Even Molly, his Molly, saw him as his father's son. Someone to love them and leave them. The only woman in Matt's life he'd ever had feelings for wasn't even giving him the choice of being involved.

'No?' She looked shocked. Pale, and beautiful.

She's really pregnant with my child.

The more he thought about it, the more protective of her he felt. Hell, he already was before this. He knew he was going to be a nightmare going forward. He felt like asking her not to leave the house till she'd given birth. He couldn't let her go, not now. He could just about cope with not having her before this, but now? What was he going to do? Watch her meet someone else, take his child with her? Hell no. He'd rather live the rest of his life taking cold showers and holding back the words he wanted to say to Molly than watch someone else live the life he was too messed-up to claim for himself.

Not for the first time, he found himself cursing both their upbringings. They were so busy trying to break the mould, they'd poured themselves right into it instead. He thought of the new life growing inside her, and he knew without a doubt he wanted to do better.

'You heard me. I know it's a shock, but my answer is no, Molly.'

Her head snapped back. 'What do you mean, no?'

'I mean no, you're not doing this on your own. *Mistake* or not.' His jaw clenched with the effort of forcing that word out. None of this was a mistake. His heritage was. 'You're having my baby. I have a say in this, whether you like it or not.'

'Okay,' she said slowly. He waited, knowing she needed to feel in control. 'What do you suggest we do then? What about working at the Ashford, and us living together?'

'Work is work. People will talk, but so what? They do anyway. I'll shut them all up. We can tell them when you're ready to, and not before. Us living together is perfect.'

'Perfect?' she echoed, looking him in the

eye. God, he wanted to draw her to him. He put his hands on his thighs to suppress the urge, felt the pressure of his nails digging into his skin.

'Yes. I have the office but we can change it to be a nursery. I barely use it.' *True. Since you moved in, I prefer to be where you are. On the couch, sitting in the garden. Cooking in the kitchen while listening to music.* 'We have the room.'

Molly was looking at him as if he had lost his mind. 'So, you want us to bring up a baby, together? Just like that?' She bit her lip. 'You need to think about this.'

'Why?' He waved his hands around. 'We already live together. We're best friends. We work together.'

She was already shaking her head. 'Exactly. Work colleagues, friends. You're talking about acting like a family! I can't ask that of you. It's not what you want.'

'You didn't ask, I'm offering and it's happening.' He tried to keep the edge from his voice, but it was there. It hung in the air between them. Stubborn? That was a normal day for Matt. When he truly wanted something, he didn't stop until he'd achieved it. He couldn't help but grind out through clenched teeth, 'Work colleagues.'

'Matt, why are you so angry?'

'I'm not angry. I just want to be there for you, Molly. This isn't some problem you can go off and deal with on your own.' He needed to box this off. To get her to agree. The panic at her turning him down was driving him mad. 'I'm all in.'

'In?' Her voice rose to match. 'In? This isn't like splitting a pizza, Matt, or even living together. Oh, God, what a mess. I had a plan.' She gripped the countertop. 'I had a plan. To save up, buy a house. Meet the guy, then have a family. The right way. This is… It's all such a mess.'

'I'm sorry,' Matt said, feeling the familiar dread in the pit of his stomach. 'I dragged you into this.'

'You didn't drag me, Matt. I knew what I was doing.' She paused. 'At least, I thought I did.' Her face flashed with pain, and he wanted to root out the cause.

'What do you mean?'

Does she regret leaving that morning like she had?

His heart jumped into his mouth.

Does she want more? Oh, God, what would I do if she does? How can I resist? How can I ever be the man she deserves?

'Nothing. It's nothing.' She sighed heavily, and Matt closed the shutters on his heart once more. 'This is serious. It's a baby. It's not something that will just go away if it doesn't work out.'

'I know that. You do know I do this for a living, right? I get how babies work.'

'Yeah.' She pushed off the stool, moving away. He rose and went with her. The two stalked around each other like magnets, attracted and repelled. 'I know that, but what about later down the line? Two years, five years. Ten? Will you still think the same then?'

'Why wouldn't I? Don't you trust me?'

'It's not that—'

'Tell me then,' he urged. Demanded. He could hear the steely tone in his own voice. Could cut the charged tension in the air between them.

'Tell you what?'

He took a step closer. 'Tell me that you trust me.' His fingers ached to reach out, to take her hand, but she looked so scared, so unsure. It was breaking his heart, and it was already damaged. Tattered. Trying to keep beating through the scars of unsaid things. Love unspoken festered in the chambers. 'Tell me that you trust me to do this.' She didn't move when he stood right in front of her, reached for her hands. Taking one of them, he moved it over her stomach, held it there with his.

'This is our baby, Molly. I never dreamed that this would happen. I'm sorry it's not the way you wanted it, the way you deserve to be a mother. You are the most important person in my life, and now there will be two. I will do anything within my power to make sure that you and our baby will never want for anything. Trust that, okay? Trust me.'

'I do trust you; I always have.' She cupped his face with her free hand. 'You really want to do this together?'

'Always,' he said. 'I told you—I'm all in.'

'He's all in? Really?' Amy was sitting aghast on the couch, her mug of tea halfway to her lips. 'Wow, Molly. I mean, I'm still reeling from the fact you had mind-blowing sex with him. Now you're his baby mama?'

'Did I say mind-blowing?' Molly blushed.

Amy nodded emphatically. 'Yes, and from the way you described it, you were still selling it short. How do you feel about all this?'

Molly sipped at her tea. 'Scared. Excited. Terrified. Elated.'

'Well, that's not confusing at all.'

'Nope. Clear as crystal.'

Confusing was a good way to describe it. She'd woken up in his bed after passing out. He'd put her into his bed instead of her own. When she'd first woken up, she had thought it might have meant something. Since they'd moved in together, she'd seen some signs of him wanting more. Or she thought she had. Hoped. Even though she'd left that note, and his bed, the memory of their time together still kept her up at night. Wondering how something so good with Matt could be such a point of misery. Even if he came to her on bended knee right now, would she even say yes? She didn't know whether to cling to him or run for the hills.

When she'd left him that note to spare him giving her the speech, she'd been hopeful all the same. She had thought that their night had meant more to him as it did her. It was so tender, so hot. He'd been so loving. Telling her she was beautiful. Talking about her body as though he'd imagined it all this time.

They'd made a baby that night, so waking in his bed once again after discovering she was pregnant seemed right. Full circle. She'd gone down the stairs to talk to him and heard him on the phone with his mother. When she'd heard what he'd said, picked up the tone of his voice, all hopes were lost.

Nothing had changed for him. He didn't want the life she wanted. He'd described it as 'white picket fence,' which sounded so twee. She didn't want a perfect cookie cutter life. She just wanted a family that didn't fall apart. The opposite of what she'd had growing up. He didn't even want to try for any of that. His childhood had sent him the other direction. A life with no ties, or people to hurt. She'd ruined it. Their one night together had scuppered both their plans. As soon as she overheard that call, she'd known for sure. Matt was doing this because he was Matt, but it didn't mean he wanted it. She'd accidentally trapped him into playing family by default, and she couldn't bear it. He felt bad for her, that she'd conceived a baby with a man who didn't want to be a family man. Neither of them was going to get their wish, but her wish was for him too. Just not like this. Nothing like this.

'He doesn't want this, you know.'

Amy frowned. 'Well, he sounds like he does to me. He cares about you. Enough to sleep with you, move you in.'

'He was being a friend, Ames.'

'You don't generally have sex with your friends.'

'I basically got tipsy and told him I fancied him from the start. I caused this,' she said sulkily.

'Er, it takes two to tango,' Amy cut in. 'He took you back to his place. He kissed you first, right?'

Molly thought of the taxi. The intense gaze on his face before he'd swooped on her in the back of that car. 'Yes.'

'Exactly! Two dance partners! You make it sound like you threw yourself at him.'

'Yeah, well. Either way, he caught me and boy does he regret it now.' She splayed one palm across her flat stomach theatrically.

'I don't think so. You've been drunk plenty of times together. You're always touchy-feely with each other. I've seen it myself. We all have. That kind of closeness doesn't come from nothing.'

'Yes, it's because we're friends! Best friends! That's all.'

Amy snorted. 'We're friends too, but I don't hug you all the time, hold your hand, kiss your forehead. The way he looks at you sometimes, it's like a romance novel.'

Molly shook her head. 'Well, even if I believed any of that, it's ruined now.' She checked her watch. 'I should be going. I said I'd meet him at home at ten. We have to go and see his mother tomorrow, sort the planning out for the wedding.'

Amy smiled and looked around at the place, empty now that their stuff was pretty much packed. 'I can't believe this is our last night here together. Look at us. I'm getting married; you're having a baby. We've come a long way.'

Molly also glanced around her, taking her old home in for the last time. 'We really have.'

Amy walked Molly to the door a short while later, where a cab was already waiting. 'Listen, cut Matt some slack. Have some faith. If he didn't want to do this, he'd tell you. He says he's all in. I for one believe him.'

Matt was waiting for her at the front door when the cab pulled up. He came down the path, then paid the driver and opened her door for her.

'Nice time? How's Amy?'

'Good. Surprised about the baby. Happy for us.'

He nodded, taking her arm in his and leading her up to the house. 'Excellent. Have you eaten?'

'Snacks. Tea.'

He frowned. 'That it?' His blue eyes looked luminescent even in the dark of the night.

'Sorry. I know, I'm fussing.' He led her inside, not letting go of her till they were both settled on the couch. She kicked off her flats, and he started to rub her feet.

'It's been two weeks since I passed out. I haven't fainted since. All the initial checks have been good. I have an excellent doctor.' That earned her a nip on the toe. 'Hey,' she laughed. 'Okay, Liam is excellent, but you're better.'

'Thank you. It doesn't stop me from worrying about you though. It's perfectly normal.' He kept saying things like that. When he took her to work, brought her lunch. Brought her folic acid and prenatal vitamins. Made her breakfast. To be fair, he'd always done most of those things. Add in the pregnancy stuff, and he was just being a good obstetrician. A great best friend. It was nice to be doted on. She felt loved, protected. Confused and horny too.

The pregnancy hormones were driving her mad, even though she knew she should have expected it. Having the knowledge and living the experience were very different, she'd realised. She could hardly be surprised either. She was living and working with Matt, knew him inside out. She knew what he looked like when he orgasmed, for God's sake! There were bound to be a few dirty thoughts on her part. He was the father. So what if she'd had the odd sexy dream about him since finding out about the baby? Like she said, hormones.

'I see you don't mind the foot rubs though,' he said teasingly.

She realised she *had* been groaning a little. Whimpering. *Oh, stop it.* She went to pull her foot away, but he held it fast.

'You ready for tomorrow?' he asked.

'The meal? Of course. I can't wait to see where Sarah's going to get married. Are you ready?' Matt scowled a little, making her laugh. 'Give over. I know you're happy for her. What's the deal with you and this wedding, really?'

He was the one to pull away this time. 'No deal. There's some leftover chilli—do you fancy some of that before bed?'

He was halfway to the kitchen already. She let him go. That was Matt. Not one to speak about his feelings, especially when it came to his mother, commitment or weddings. Fair enough. She did need to ask him one thing about Sarah's wedding though. She'd definitely be showing by then. Not easy to hide the fact she was pregnant.

'Are you taking a date with you on the

day?' She heard a bowl clatter to the floor. 'Matt, you okay?'

'Yeah,' he called back after a string of expletives. 'Dropped a dish. Are you?'

'Am I what?'

He was back before she knew it, holding two steaming bowls of chilli. Grated cheese sitting on top, hunks of buttered bread on a side plate resting on his wrist.

'Taking a date to the wedding. I thought we'd go together.' He passed her a dish, then half slammed the plate of bread onto the coffee table.

Okay, that was weird.

'Well, I did too, but I just thought I'd ask because…you know.' She pointed to her stomach.

His face was blank. 'The baby?' He raised a brow. He was smiling, but it didn't reach his eyes. 'Well, I don't think the baby will take up much space, if you're worried about too many plus-ones on the invite. We were already going together. That's not changed for me.'

He spooned some chilli into his mouth, chewing like a lion on a gazelle leg.

'Me neither. It's just… Are you ready for the questions? Your mum's friends are all going to be there. Family too.'

He looked relieved. 'That's it? There's no problem with that. You know my mum already knows. I told her the day we found out.'

'Yes.' But she'd spoken to Sarah in the days since, and she'd never mentioned a word about it. Ever the diplomat. He was more like his mother than he realised, she mused with a smile. Shame he thought his father had a hold on him too. She knew that would be troubling him. Having a baby, especially like this.

She finally got the courage to ask, 'Don't you care what people will say? Us there together, me with a pregnant belly?'

'I'll never be ashamed or embarrassed by our child, Molly. We will be there together.' His jaw flexed. He swallowed before he answered. She heard it. 'No one will say a thing to you while I'm around.'

Molly's heart swelled. Ever the protector. The thought of being there together, watching his mother get married, their baby on the way... It was almost perfect. She thought of what Amy had said. God, she wished it was true, but she'd overheard that phone call he'd had with his mum. It was what she constantly came back to whenever she allowed herself to want more. She wished she could tell him she didn't long for the perfect life. The white picket fence wasn't it at all. She just wanted to feel the way he made her feel. Safe. Loved. Seen.

'What about you?' He brought her attention back with his soft probing voice.

'What about me? It's your family. I'm not embarrassed at all.'

'They're your family too,' he chided. 'You know my mum loves you. She's thrilled, by the way. She's been biting her tongue every time she spoke to you since she found out, in case you didn't want to discuss it with her yet. She's been hard to hold off, to be honest.'

Molly blushed. 'I'll talk to her tomorrow,' she promised. She thought he'd be happy, but his still-furrowed brow was unmistakable. 'That wasn't what you meant, was it?'

'No.' He looked away, focusing on anything but her. 'I don't want you to feel…bad.'

'Bad?'

'My reputation,' he supplied reluctantly. He looked like he wanted the ground to swallow him up. 'My mum's friends, they knew my father too. Some of them are still in touch with him. He deals with their cases. You know what that circle is like.'

She could feel the rage simmering in him. It came off him in waves whenever he talked about his dad. Without thinking about it, she went to him. The bowls sat discarded on the coffee table now, and she was up on the couch, on her knees. He turned to her, surprise registering on his face.

'Stop that. Now. I mean it, Matt.'

'Stop what?'

She took his face in her hands, was so close to him that she could just pucker up and they'd be kissing. He'd straightened his body, pushing himself even closer to her.

Magnets, she thought.

The proximity of him was intoxicating. They'd well and truly broken the touch barrier now. Again. She missed him. The way she used to fall asleep in his arms watching the TV. They were slowly getting it back, but it would never be enough now.

'Molly, what are you doing?'

'I hate it when you do that. I never knew your dad, sure. I never want to know him. I do know your mother though, and you are so like her. All the good things. This front you insist on putting up, it's infuriating. You don't have to worry about me feeling any kind of shame being seen out with you.' She took his hand, putting it back on her stomach before returning hers to cup his gorgeous face. She could feel the warmth of his touch through her top. Feel his fingers rub her tummy affectionately.

'This might not be the plan I had for my life,' she continued, 'but so what? I was hardly dating Prince Charming, was I? I was floundering, outside of work. This baby...' She smiled, thinking of the life growing inside her. 'Our baby, it's a good thing. I don't regret that.' She leaned in closer to touch her forehead to his. 'I don't regret you being the father. I'm grateful for it.'

Matt let out a breath, as though he'd been holding it the whole time. 'You mean that?' he half whispered, moving his hands to settle around her waist. She caught a whiff of his cologne, and the butterflies flew loose again. Fluttering around them both as they gazed at each other. 'You're glad it's me?'

'Matt,' she said, exasperated. 'Always.'

Is that it? Could that be it? He thinks he's his father's son?

Perhaps it wasn't the stupid white-fence scenario that scared him. Maybe, just maybe, it was the thought of not being able to keep it once he had it. Involving her and his child in the juggernaut of gossip that swirled around him until he feared she'd leave him. Fear. Fear of loss. Fear of not doing the right thing. Falling flat on his face in front of the people who had judged him all his life regardless. She could show him otherwise. Right now, she wanted to show him a lot of things.

His pupils dilated under her scrutiny. She was breathing harder, faster, and she could see his chest heaving under his clothes. Maybe it was the hormones, the smell of him. The feel of him pulling her closer with his muscular arms. Their talk. Or just…them. Whatever it was, she needed him.

'Kiss me,' she begged. His eyes widened. 'Kiss me, Matt. Please.'

He looked conflicted, and she made a bold move before he had a chance to think about it.

Her lips were on his before he finished saying her name. She kissed at his closed mouth, feeling him tense. Just before she pulled back, lost her nerve, his mouth opened. His tongue licked at her lips. She sent hers to meet it, deepening the kiss and moving closer. She ended up sitting astride him, her knees on the outside of his thighs. She could feel his ardour through his trousers, and it spurred her on.

He wants this. Wants me.

His arms were pulling her tighter now, hands roving under her top. One flick of his wrist and her bra clasp came loose. She mewled, not caring how obviously aroused she was. He seemed to love it, his hands coming around to the front. Cupping her breasts.

'God,' he almost roared, his voice deep. The gravel in his tone rumbled around her. 'Pregnancy agrees with you.'

He pulled back, and for a second she thought the mention of the baby had pulled him out of it.

'Don't stop,' she urged, pushing her chest towards him. He looked so turned on, yet so conflicted. 'Please, don't stop.'

'Are you sure? What about—'

'Doctor, I think you know the answer to that. It's fine. I want this.' She ground herself shamelessly onto his lap, and his responding moan thrilled her. 'I want you.'

Before she could catch her breath, she was up off the couch. His lips were back on hers, his strong arms under her backside, holding her in place as he walked towards the staircase. She grabbed on to him with her hands, her thighs. Cupping his face, kissing his sexy chiselled face off as he mounted the stairs. His stairs were in two parts, and when they got to the top of the landing, he pushed her against the wall, as if he couldn't bear to take the next little flight without getting more.

'My Molly,' he whispered, running his stubble down her neck as he kissed his way to her collarbone. He pulled back, but she felt solid, supported in his hands. He nudged his head towards her top.

'Take it off,' he commanded. She locked her blue eyes on to his, absentmindedly hoping for a second that the colours of their eyes would merge into their child's. She focused on the hue of his irises as she took the material between her fingers. His hands were clasped firmly on her bottom, her back leaning against the painted wall he'd pushed her up against. She slowly pulled the top over her head, taking her unstrapped bra with it. Matt made a deep, visceral noise from the back of his throat, burying his head between her pregnancy-swollen breasts. Kissing and licking the exposed skin between them.

'I like them like this.' He kissed one nipple, then made it pucker as he blew on it. 'They were perfect before, but now...' He kissed the other as she threw her clothing aside. It landed on the banister. 'Amazing,' he breathed. 'You take my breath away.'

He drew back, and they were on the move again. His motions pushed his groin into hers, making her eyes roll back in her head from the sensations. He kicked open his bedroom door, as if he'd never even considered taking her to her own bed. She felt a surge of fresh lust. She wanted to be back in his bed. Had wanted it every night since she'd moved her things in.

She expected him to put her down, lay her on his bed, but he turned. Sat down on the edge and took her with him. She went to grab his T-shirt from his back, and he pulled away just enough to let her remove it. He seemed disappointed at having to lift his hands from her body. The second she'd undressed his torso, he gripped her waist. Tight, possessive. Soft and tender. All at the same time. He gave her a look that made her libido spike off the chart. Like he wanted to utterly ruin her and worship her all at the same time. It was intoxicating. They looked at each other, as if time and space had stopped. Like it meant nothing, because they were here together. In this moment.

'You drive me crazy,' he muttered. 'I don't know what to do when I'm around you lately. I can't think straight. I don't want to lose you.' He looked a little sad about it, and she wanted to know why, what this beautiful man was thinking, but she didn't want him to pull away from her. Not now. Not ever.

'You won't.' He didn't look convinced. 'Matt, you could never lose me.' His half smile was a nice little reward, but she knew he needed to hear more. She couldn't shake off that phone call though, what he'd said to his mum when he thought she was sleeping. It wasn't the time. She couldn't say the words.

'Let me make you feel good,' she said instead. Using his own words to reach him, like he had her. A little code of theirs. She took charge. Reached down to cup him. To show him what she could do. 'I want this, Matt.' She was sailing so close to the truth now. To everything she wanted to say but wasn't ready to divulge yet. 'I want you.'

She touched her lips to his, the softest and tenderest of kisses. She put everything she wanted to say into that kiss. Actions speaking far louder than the words she was holding back. There was no fear in her touch. No hesitation, or embarrassment. She could show him how she felt this way, and for now at least it would be enough. She would worry about the consequences later. She couldn't stay away from him. She'd already failed. The way he took her in his arms, kissed her back, she had an inkling that he couldn't either. He reached for her, discarding any clothing that got in his way, and she stopped herself from overthinking. From thinking at all. By the time he entered her, she was already about to climax again. She gripped his shoulders tight, whispering his name feverishly as he thrust into her, her name on his lips like a promise.

CHAPTER ELEVEN

MATT LOREN WAS a one-woman man. As they got out of his Lexus, hand in hand walking towards the fancy hotel his mother was getting married in later that year, the thought popped into his head.

That's a lie. His brain laughed back at him. *The thought didn't just pop into your head. It's always been there.*

True, he agreed with himself, grinning back at Molly as she smiled up at him.

Man, if my dad could see me now.

Matt liked to think it would irk him. That his son was trying to be the man he never was.

'You ready for this?'

'Are you?' he teased. 'You look a little tired.' Her smile turned from wholesome to sexy in half a second.

'Yeah, well. Someone kept me awake.'

He winked at her, which made her sexy smile all the brighter.

God almighty, she is stunning.

They'd woken up in his bed, naked. Limbs entwined around each other. Her little spoon bum making him hard as soon as she started to stir. He didn't tell her, but he'd been awake for a while. Watching her sleep. Wondering how he could be so close to having it all, and so undeserving. At times like this, he was jealous of his mother. Getting to shed the Loren name. He almost hoped that Molly would insist on their child taking her surname, but not enough to suggest it. He still needed that connection. He just wished her surname would be the same too. Possessive? Probably. He felt like a stud dog, wanting to mark his territory, chase off any other contenders.

He'd made love to her again that morning, a slow, leisurely push of his hips into her body. Her once-sleepy eyes rolling with pleasure as he rubbed his thumb against her clitoris, no need for talking. *Is this what a relationship is like? I could never go back to meaningless sex after this.* They'd spent half the night together like that. Touching each other, tasting. He literally could not get enough of her. Even now, walking into the hotel, he had to adjust himself, his erection painful against his tailored trousers.

'You okay?' She squeezed his fingers in hers. 'Where did you go then?'

Into you, he thought. *I was deep into you.*

'Nowhere,' he said, squeezing her hand back and willing his hard-on to go away. 'Just thinking about last night.'

Nice going, idiot. Now you're thinking about her naked breasts again. About how nice it would be to wake up next to her every morning. Not a wall apart.

She smirked, lifting onto the balls of her feet to whisper something into his ear. They were nearly at the entrance, and he didn't want to come in his boxers. He turned his head and dropped a quick peck onto her cheek. He hated himself for the look of disappointment on her face but needs must. She was driving him wild, and he couldn't shut himself off like he did with every other woman he'd been with.

'Let's find my mother, yes?'

She nodded, a faint flush colouring her cheeks.

Damn it, now she felt rejected.

He flexed his fingers, wrapping hers tighter in between them. He felt her relax as they headed inside.

'Hello, you two!' Duncan and Sarah were waiting in the foyer, a glass of champagne in each of their hands. 'What do you think? Beautiful grounds.'

Duncan looked nervous. Matt stepped forward without letting go of Molly, offering his free hand.

'Gorgeous,' he said, even though on the way in he hadn't paid much attention. 'Nice to see you again.' Duncan's nervous smile dissipated. Molly let go of his hand, and he mourned the loss.

'So.' He distracted himself by making small talk as he watched Molly walk across to the bar area with his mother. They were deep in conversation. His eyes never left Molly. 'How are the nerves? Getting cold feet yet?'

Duncan laughed. 'Not a chance. I wish it was sooner. Still a few weeks to wish away yet. What about you?'

'Me what?' His mother was embracing Molly now. The news of the baby was official, it seemed.

'Are you ready to walk your mother down the aisle?'

He turned to Duncan and realised that the man had been watching him watch Molly all along. 'No, no nerves here. Shall we get a drink?'

'Good idea,' Duncan agreed. 'Scotch, is it? Or too early?'

'Driving,' Matt replied. 'We have to get back tonight, as we're working tomorrow. I'll take a soft drink though.' He was hot on Duncan's heels, eager to follow Molly to the bar. His heartbeat raced when he saw her face light up the minute she realised he was at her side again. He wanted to reach out, wrap his arms around her, but there was a little crowd at the bar. He wasn't sure how she would react. She answered him by lacing her arm through his, reaching up to drop a kiss on his cheek. When he looked at his mother, he could see that she was positively vibrating with happiness.

'Thanks both of you for coming. They are pretty packed here over the next few weeks, so I wanted to take the time to do the planning, run through the day. Having lunch and tasting the menu at the same time seemed perfect.'

A waiter appeared, pristine black and white uniform denoting the character of the place. It was nice to see his mother getting a touch of some opulence for once. It made the years of struggling seem worth it somehow. 'Your table is ready, if your party has all arrived?'

* * *

Lunch was perfect. Duncan's younger brother, Edward was just like him. Kind, funny. It was annoying, if Matt was honest. Edward loved Molly from the off, which wasn't surprising. Everyone did.

She was glowing today. She'd put on a dress he'd not seen before for the outing. A gorgeous blue that seemed familiar to him somehow. The shade reminded him of something. It brought out the darker blue in her eyes. Made her blond hair almost ice-white. She was radiant. Flushed from the pregnancy, and the morning sex. He was already looking forward to them being alone again. After their morning session, they'd drifted back to sleep. Had woken in a panic, realising that they were late for the two-hour drive to the venue his mother had picked for the wedding.

Duncan's family lived in the North, so they'd settled on somewhere halfway in between. That was his mother, always thinking about everyone else. He'd already booked him and Molly a twin room for the event. He was tempted to ask them to change it to a double while he was here but he didn't want to presume, even after last night. They'd not discussed it. Molly had fallen asleep in the car pretty much the second they'd hit the road.

He'd let her sleep. She was growing their child; she needed the rest. Talking about what came next could wait.

His mother had been watching them for most of the meal; he could feel her eyes on them. Every time Molly reached for him or gave him a little smile. Told the table one of their work stories, holding back the client details but keeping the humour and warmth of the situations they'd found themselves in. The baby wasn't mentioned, and he loved his mother for not putting him on the spot. He realised that Duncan knew as well, but he found he wasn't bothered by it. Far from it. Duncan seemed pleased too, and he felt an odd sense of pride. Was this what it was like to be in love, starting a family and sharing the news with your own parents?

Damn, just listen to yourself. You'll be calling Duncan Dad next. Simpering over Babygros and stuffed toys. Although...we do need to get going on that side of things.

The rest of the afternoon was relaxed, fun even. Matt felt as though something had eased. Being in public together like that had offered real insight into how things were on the other side of the track.

They were driving home now, having been waved off by his mother and Duncan. Molly had been quiet since they'd left, looking out of the window. Her hands were in her lap, and she kept picking at the skin on the sides of her manicured fingers. She'd had them done especially for today, he'd noted. Work called for short unpolished nails. He was absurdly happy that she'd made such an effort. As if she really cared.

'Well, that was a lot easier than I expected.' He tried to start up a conversation. All he got was a distracted smile and a nod, and her face was back at the window. 'Do you have anything planned for the rest of today?'

She looked at him then, intrigued. 'No, I was just planning to have a bath and an early-ish night. Back to work tomorrow.'

He nodded, noticing for the first time how tired she looked underneath her make-up. He felt bad for being the cause. 'No problem. We'll just go straight home.'

Her eyes didn't leave him. 'What did you have in mind?'

The place they stopped at, near to home, was like a baby superstore. Matt had never seen so much equipment, all seemingly put into three realms. Pink, blue and anything bland to pass for either. Gender neutrality hadn't quite caught up when it came to babies, it seemed. At the hospital, they didn't assign colours to any of the babies as such. Boy or girl, they were put in blankets and clothes of all colours. He was pleased to think about it. Not every girl wanted pink, nor every boy wanted blue. Even he knew that, from his limited experience of children.

'Wow,' Molly exclaimed from his side. 'Where the heck do we start?'

She'd readily agreed to look at baby things on the way home. All her tests had been normal, Molly was carrying well and the pregnancy was perfect so far. She was over two months, so it made sense. Plus, given the fact that she was still looking for flat listings, Matt figured that showing her how the baby could fit in at his house was a good idea. He hated the thought of Molly not being there when he woke up. Even if she was in another room. He already felt so protective over her and the baby. He needed them to stay with him. Maybe she would agree to it if she saw the baby's room all kitted-out. Ready for them to tackle the challenge. Together.

Matt took a deep breath. 'Well, we'll need a cot, so let's start there.' He took her hand in his, and she allowed him to lead her over to the back wall. There was an array of differently coloured wooden cots in various sizes and styles. Some were dressed up already, cot bumper sets with bunny rabbits or bears or hot-air balloons.

'Wow.' Molly's voice was flat, unimpressed. 'The ducks are a bit scary, aren't they?' She poked a hanging duck soft toy from one of the mobiles. 'They look dead-eyed. I wouldn't fancy staring at them every night. Don't they have anything else?'

Matt tore his gaze from a weird looking animal cot bumper. It looked like a family of dead racoons from a distance, pretending to be pretty little teddy bears.

'Like what?' he quipped. 'Little stethoscopes?' He squeezed her hand. She squeezed it back.

This is nice. Domesticated.

'Hi there, can I be of any help?' The pair turned to see a woman in staff uniform behind them. Her name badge declared her to be a 'Baby Expert' called Priscilla. Matt saw Molly's eyes narrow when she read the label. He resisted the urge to laugh. He was pretty sure Molly had the slight edge on the 'baby expert' tag. Maybe he'd make her a joke one for work.

'Er…no, th—'

'Yes,' Matt cut Molly off. 'We do actually. We need to kit out a nursery.'

I need it to be enticing, homely. Somewhere Molly can picture laying our child to sleep.

The woman beamed. 'Well, you've come to the right place. Mr…?'

'Loren, but call me Matt, please. This is Molly.'

Molly was already smiling at her, but she looked uncomfortable. Luckily, the saleswoman had no issues in filling the silence.

'Matt, Molly, we have you covered. So, just so I have a guide…on budget, timescale? Is this your first baby?'

'Yes, my first,' Molly replied. 'I think we'll just start with some of the smaller things. Car seat, maybe? I would like one to fit into a pram. Maybe this one?' She was already off, heading to the area that housed the prams. The woman gave Matt a weird look, probably as confused as he was.

My first. Not our first.

It was probably nothing, a slip of the tongue, but it still stung him. His phone rang in his pocket, and he was in two minds. Did he go and stake his claim? Go over there and casually mention it was his baby too? Why did he feel so hurt that even a shop assistant didn't know the truth? He was trying to care for Molly, be protective of her, but it was clear

she didn't want or need him. He answered
the call.

'Hello, Dr Loren.'

It was the Ashford on the line, and he had
to go immediately. An emergency.

'I'm on my way,' he answered grumpily. A
young sales assistant passed him, a stack of
boxes in the lad's hand. Matt rushed over to
him, no time to lose.

'Do me a favour.' He pointed over to the
two women. 'Tell that blonde customer Matt
had to leave for work. An emergency, okay?
Tell her I'm sorry and ask her to take a cab
home. She'll understand!'

He was already out of the door when the
boy turned around, taking the ear bud out of
his ear.

'What did you say? Sir?'

Molly.

He'd left her there, right in the middle of the
stupid baby superstore. Looking like a total
idiot. She'd called Matt's name, looked for
him. She'd had to arrange a cab home and that
was only after buying half the shop too out
of sheer embarrassment. Her credit card was
still smoking, unaccustomed to being used,
never mind being taken on a spree.

One minute he was there, the next gone. No

phone call, no text. He'd just walked right out of the place. She'd come home to find his car missing. His place in darkness.

The cab driver had taken pity on her and brought the boxes in for her. 'First baby, eh?'

'Er…yeah,' she said, raiding her purse for a tip. 'Thought I'd better make a start.' She passed him the money. 'Even as a midwife, I didn't realise that they needed so much.'

He chuckled. 'I remember. We only had a small flat when we started out.' He glanced at the photo on Matt's side table. It showed the two of them on New Year's Eve. It was one of her favourite photos. A guys-and-dolls party a friend had thrown. Matt had let his hair down that night for once, really laughing and having fun with the others, and not just her. His fake tommy gun rested under one of his arms, Molly held in his other. They were both laughing into the camera. She could still remember the moment. He'd seen the photographer coming and lunged for her.

Come here, he'd said, kissing her cheek as she squealed in his arms. *I can't have a photo without my girl.*

The driver saw her gaze at the photo. 'Well.' He smiled. 'You two just enjoy it. It goes so fast.'

'Oh, we're…' She should have put him

straight, but she didn't. She didn't want to explain to anyone how they weren't together. Why they weren't. She didn't really understand it herself. The longer she was here with Matt, doing this, the more it would make her want it. She didn't know how they'd got here, but she couldn't bring herself to regret it. Not the nights together, and definitely not the baby.

Once she'd closed the door on the driver, she took a shower. Dressed in sweats, she came back down to the packages. She'd half expected Matt to be back by now, sitting in his chair reading, making something to eat in the kitchen. It was too quiet without him. She'd dialled his number, but only got his voicemail. His phone was only turned off for work. She rang the Ashford, asking if he was on shift.

'Dr Loren's here, dealing with an emergency, yes. Do you have a message you want to pass on?'

'No, no.' She got off the call as quickly as she could. The last thing she wanted getting round was that she'd phoned looking for him. She and Matt didn't do that. They normally knew, so didn't need to check in. He'd just walked out of that store without a second thought. For all she knew, he'd panicked in there, and left her. The emergency could have come after, saving him from having to explain. Why else would he just leave her there without a word?

Hell, now I'm trying to work out what was going on in his head.

She never had to do that before. He was the one man in her life whom she didn't need to be wary of or worry about.

She flicked on the television and made herself a sandwich. After she'd eaten and tried to distract herself with a reality show, she gave up. Pulling one of the large brown paper bags towards her, she started to unpack the tiny clothes she'd bought that day. She'd picked pretty trendy designs, nothing too cutesy. She could tell from Matt's face he'd thought the same as her about the flopsy bunnies and eerie-looking teddy bears. She didn't want to kit the baby out that way. Something simple, classic. Nothing too cute. She was pretty sure Matt had never been a baby anyway. He must have arrived into the world with a determined scowl on his face.

Maybe they'd make this work, maybe not. They'd had sex again. A lot of sex. Wow, it'd been even better than last time. It felt as though he'd wanted to be there, with her. Like she was the only person in the world. Like the first time, but that it meant even more. He'd held her tighter, whispered sweet nothings into her ear, as though his tongue had been loosened and now he couldn't stop telling her how he felt. In the morning though, nothing. He wasn't weird per se, but he wasn't exactly forthcoming either. He didn't mention anything that had happened, just spoke of their day. Which had gone well, until he took her to buy baby things and then bolted on her.

Molly made a stack of the clothes and went to write everything down. An inventory. After she'd moved around so much growing up, it was something she always did. Once that was done, she turned the notepad to a clean page. Started writing something else.

She'd always done well on her own. Before Matt, she firmly believed that people were just human beings she would have to encounter in life as she went about hers. Before the Ashford, before she grew to love Amy, before she met Matt, she was firmly of that resolve. Once it was meant to happen, it would. She'd find love. The one person she could trust beyond all reason, and love enough to let in. The small nugget of hope that she held, kept close to her chest. All of that felt so close now but altered. Imperfect. Like there was a crucial piece or two still missing. Molly didn't like feeling out of control, and she wanted to try taking it back. She couldn't talk to Matt about it, and Amy was busy. So she wrote to her child instead, using the nickname she'd formed for their unborn babe.

Little Resident,

I know it's a strange name to call you, but your daddy is a doctor, your mama is a midwife and you might be one day too. Since you're residing in me at the moment, it kinda fits.

I don't even know why I'm writing this. I think it's for me more than for you, my tiny peanut. You've caused all kinds of trouble already, but that's not your fault.

I know things are messed-up right now, but I want to make you a promise. Here and now. Reassure you of a few things too.

Your father is the best. Literally. My best friend. The best doctor I've ever known. He's the best son to your grandma, and he'll be the best dad. He doesn't think that, but that's your daddy. He never sees what I see, and maybe one day you can show him just how amazing he is.

Just bear with him. He might need a minute now and again to get on the same page.

Your dad and I didn't have the easiest start in life. Our parents were...complicated. It made me independent and your dad stubborn. Guarded. We won't always get it right, but the point is, little one, we will be here. For you. To love you. Fiercely. Unconditionally. For ever.

Whatever happens, my child, I can promise you two parents who will never stop doing everything they can to make you happy. To keep you safe. To keep each other safe. To love you fiercely, just as we love each other.

Always.

Love you, baby.

Mummy

She'd gone to bed right after stacking the baby's things up in her room. She left her notepad on top, figuring she could show the list to Matt later. Maybe he'd want to go back to the store with her, save the delivery driver bothering.

When she'd woken up, it was morning. Matt's car still wasn't there. His bed was still rum-

pled from the night they'd spent together.
Her phone was devoid of messages. He'd not
checked in, at home or on her phone.

Well, that's your answer.

He'd obviously not changed that much.
She headed to work in a fog, barely remembering the bus ride to the Ashford. She went
to get changed, slamming her locker shut in
frustration. The nausea was gone now, but she
still felt sick to her stomach. She was desperate to see Matt this morning, but she hated
herself for it. She'd already texted Amy, asking her if she fancied catching up after work.
She didn't fancy an awkward night at Chez
Loren.

She slammed her locker again, just for
something to do. She had fifteen minutes till
the beginning of her shift, but she wasn't in a
rush to get to handover. She'd seen what life
would be like living with Matt, raising a child
together. They'd fallen at the first damned
hurdle. Standing there holding a deformed
stuffed dog in that store, she'd wondered
whether Matt was really capable of being
there for her.

She didn't like the feeling of going it alone
now as much as she'd thought she would.
She'd had her first glimpse of life as a single
mother, doing things on her own. She could

do it, she knew, but with Matt there? Wondering whether he resented them both? Wishing he was with someone else? She'd considered that too. She couldn't lie and say it hadn't crossed her mind. That he'd just leave them to go and hook up with someone. He was technically single, after all. Would still be single when the baby was here. She fixed an errant lock of hair that had escaped from her tight ponytail, checking herself over. Trying to bring some semblance of control to herself. She needed order, and work.

'Morning!' George trilled as she got to the nurses' station.

'Good morning,' Molly said, too busy looking at the boards behind him to notice her friend gawking at her. 'What have we got today?'

'Well, we had quite the trauma last night,' Liam said from behind her. Molly turned to see he and Matt both standing there, looking exhausted. 'Room Three, Caroline Sellers. Had twins via Caesarean section last night. Both babies are doing well, thirty-four weeks and three days delivery.'

Matt came and stood at her side. She felt his fingers brush her hand, and she crossed her arms across her chest before she took them in hers. He frowned, moving a fraction closer. She moved back, away from him, pretending to look at the board with a little more scrutiny even though she already knew what it said. Liam was still talking to the rest of the team about the operation.

'Are you okay?' Matt grazed his side against hers, but she kept her arms folded. 'Sorry I didn't get a chance to call you after I left the shop. I tried, but my stupid phone had died. I forgot to charge it the night before.'

The fact that he hadn't put his phone on charge because he was too busy taking her to bed didn't need saying, but Molly was clicking the pieces into place. He'd been at work the whole time, and he'd tried to call her. She felt herself thaw a little, but the seed of doubt had already been sown there. In her head. She didn't want to be the one who was always calling the hospital to see if he was there. Sure, he was there for her now, attentive. What about when their baby was born— would the novelty wear off? He had needs, after all, and they weren't a couple.

'Molly?' He'd turned to her now. 'Are you angry with me?'

'Yes,' she half hissed. 'Not now, okay?'

'Yes now,' he retorted, not lowering his voice one iota. 'I'm sorry I didn't call you.'

'You left me in the shop!'

Liam looked their way, but Matt didn't even flinch. He reached for her hands, and she brushed him off. Checked to see if anyone was watching. They were all getting on with their work, which was just what she was supposed to be doing.

'I told the stock boy to tell you I had a work emergency and to catch a cab home; did he not tell you?' When Molly shook her head, Matt looked as if he wanted to go back and murder him. He cursed under his breath several times before visibly composing himself. 'Molly, I'm sorry. I did ask him to tell you. My phone is never usually dead, you know that. Did you get anything from the shop?'

She nodded stiffly. 'Yeah, I got a few things. They're in my room if you want to look. You don't have to be sorry,' she added, pretending that she didn't give a jot about where he'd been. 'You don't owe me an explanation for your whereabouts. We're not together. The baby's not here yet.'

She walked away and joined George while Liam and the head midwife on the night shift were discussing the patients on the ward, what procedures were scheduled for the day, what clinics were running. Matt went and stood beside Liam, but his eyes were locked on Molly the whole time.

'What's his deal?' George whispered out the side of his mouth. 'You two had a fight?'

'Something like that,' Molly half whispered back. George waved to Matt, who realised he'd been spotted and glanced away. 'Stop it!'

'Hey,' George countered. 'I'll have you know that over the last few weeks, your man and I have got along a little better.'

'Really,' Molly dead-panned. 'Best buddies, eh?'

George stifled a laugh. 'No, but he has been a lot nicer. All the staff have said the same thing.'

Matt was staring at her again, and she glared right back this time. A smile tugged at his features, till he shut it down and continued looking at her intently. As if he could make her less mad by just staring her anger down. She ignored him. She was annoyed with him.

All the staff have said the same thing.

George's words pinballed around her skull.

'Really, he's been nice to everyone?'

'I know,' George murmured. 'We couldn't believe it either, but to be honest... I quite like him now.'

'You what?'

She said it a little too loud, and the surrounding conversations dropped from a low ebb to a pin-dropping silence.

'Something to share, Molly? Before we get to work?' Liam's brow was raised, but she didn't get a sense of irritation from him. More like mild amusement. At his side, Matt was positively smirking. He couldn't have known what they were talking about, but he'd probably worked out it involved him.

As she glanced around her, the mood did seem quieter somehow. Calmer. Less tense, even with Matt looking every inch the surly doctor he normally was. 'No, no. Nothing to add, Doctor.'

'Are you sure?' Matt's voice cut across the room. 'Nothing else?'

What is he doing?

She was about to shake her head, say no, when she saw his eyes dip to her stomach.

The baby? He wanted her to declare it to everyone, right here?

She raised her brows in question at him, but he raised them right back. Tilted his head with a tiny nod.

Is he...challenging me?

She thought about what his angle might be. He was wanting her to tell their news, here. With him there.

Maybe, just maybe, this was his way of

being there for her. Everyone was looking at her like she was about to drop some truth bomb. The second truth bomb of the week.

He'd already told her that he'd notified HR about their relationship. He'd gone and declared them to be living together, with a baby on the way. They had to, given their working hours and HR requirements. The Ashford HR department apparently didn't even react. When Matt had relayed the conversation back to her, she'd read in between the lines. Although HR had these rules, either they highly valued the pair of them working together and wouldn't rock that boat—or they'd thought that the relationship was already there in some way or another.

George elbowed her in the side, bringing her back out of her head and into the room with all the tension.

'Sorry.' She smiled at everyone, looking at no one. 'It's nothing.'

She studied Matt, expecting him to be laughing or smirking, but his face...

She realised what he was doing under the bravado of his usual pushing. His challenge. He'd told HR, and now he wanted her to tell everyone. She thought of what George had said, about him making the effort at work.

She'd not really noticed, already knowing the true, full picture of Matthew Loren.

That's what he's been showing them. Himself. He's been trying, this whole time.

She locked eyes with him, saw his tight, grim jawline clench, and the words came easily. The crowd had already started to disperse, to get to the day.

'I do have some news.' Molly stopped them all. She smiled as she thought of what she was about to tell them. It was good news. Exciting. 'I'm pregnant.' She moved from George's side, taking in his open mouth, and the faces of her other colleagues, as she went to stand next to Matt. The minute she was near him, he reached for her hand, pulling her to him. 'Matt and I are having a baby.' His hand gripped tighter when she spoke his name. She could see George's face, close to exploding with shock and surprise, and looked up at Matt.

This time, his expression was one she'd seen only a few times, and had searched for ever since. After they'd first lain in bed together. When they were sitting on the sofa, watching the television and talking about baby names. He looked down at her with such peace, his face was serene.

He'd begged her with his eyes to tell the

people in their lives about their child, but this…this was like declaring they were to-gether too. She just…had to test the theory. Do what she always did, match his stake and up the ante. What she was doing was dangerous, but she couldn't live in limbo. She had to know.

As if he knew what was going through her head, he finally reacted as people around them came out of their stupors to congratulate them. He brought their clasped hands up to his face, rubbing them against the hard stubble on his cheek, then kissed her hand. Just two soft, short little pecks. Comfortable, like they'd done it for ever. Pulling back, Molly managed to see his calm smile broaden before George was in her face.

'Molly! You're having a baby! Really?' He was stunned but beaming his head off. 'O-M-G, does Amy know? How do you feel? How many weeks?'

She laughed, feeling Matt's hand slide out of hers as George and a couple of her other colleagues took her off to dissect the news. When she looked back, he was already walking down the corridor, deep in conversation with Liam.

Before she knew it, they were back to the job. Everyone knew about the baby she was having with Matt, and she was working away as normal. After she delivered her second healthy baby of the day, she realised that she felt happy. Settled. Like a weight had been lifted off her shoulders. She couldn't wait to see what happened next. Maybe they really did have this thing all sorted out.

'Ready?' she asked, grinning, when she got to the main doors of the Ashford that evening. Matt was in his usual spot, leaning against one of the pillars like he was shooting a *GQ* cover. She felt her stomach flip at the sight of him.

'Not quite,' he returned, taking her into his arms and slipping the handbag off her shoulder to carry himself. 'I need to nip back in. Come with me?'

Her feet were killing her, but she nodded anyway. 'If you're quick, I had visions of a hot soapy bath in my near future.'

They walked towards the consultation rooms, and just before he opened the door to Room Four, he whispered into her ear. 'I have a vision of that too now. I might just have to get my loofah out.'

She chuckled, following him into the room. 'Promises, promises.' He motioned to the bed in the corner. 'What?'

He was smiling, but she could see his nerves hiding behind it.

'Don't be mad. I know you have an ultrasound booked, but I thought for the first time... Well, we have all these machines.' He pressed his lips together. 'I wanted it to be just us. What do you say?'

Molly was already heading towards the bed, his hand in hers.

'I think it's a great idea. Are you really ready?'

His smile dipped, and she hated herself for second-guessing him.

If he's not ready, he wouldn't be doing it, she chided herself.

'I'm ready,' he said. 'Let's meet the little one, eh?'

The gel on her belly was colder than she'd expected. She felt a pang of guilt for her patients; she'd never realised it was such a jolt. She only saw the joy of the scans, or the horror of finding something awful on the screen and having to break the news. It hit a lot differently when it was your stomach, your baby.

'I'm scared,' she admitted. 'Pathetic, eh?'

Matt shook his head, his hand holding the instrument an inch from contact. She noticed the slight shake and felt better.

'No, baby,' he soothed. 'Not at all.' He took her hand in his, around the instrument.

'No peeking,' she said urgently, realising that on the screen the baby might show them more than she wanted to know. 'At the sex, I mean. I know it's too early anyway, but—'

He laughed. 'Spoil-sport. But I'm not that good.'

Her sceptical brow raise had him chuckling again.

'Okay, fair point. No peeking.' He leaned down and spoke to her stomach. 'You listening in there, little peanut? Cross your legs.'

Her laughter made her tummy jiggle, the gel wobbling.

'Ready?'

Their eyes locked, both of them taking in the moment before pushing on.

Is this how every parent-to-be feels? It's worrying, terrifying, scary. Elating, exciting, daunting. I'd run out of adjectives to describe this moment and still not do it justice.

'Let's do it,' she said.

Together their hands pushed down, made contact with the gel. Matt had turned the screen away from her, like they always did for patients. She found herself holding her breath as Matt's eyes roved over it. When he broke out into a broad grin, she relaxed.

When the screen turned, Molly had to remind herself to breathe. The black and white image was clear. Healthy. Everything where it should be, right on track. Teeny, fragile, but there. A scrap of life, made from love. Molly felt like her throat was blocked off and she was unable to speak. A single tear rolled down her cheek.

'I can't believe that's our baby,' Matt uttered, his voice a half-cracked whisper. He reached up and pointed to the tiny little flutter on the screen. 'Strong heart, just like his mama,' he said, and she saw that face again. The serene look she'd grown to crave seeing. 'Hello, baby.' He leaned in and dropped a kiss right above the gel. 'I love you so much.' His smile dimmed when he saw Molly's face.

'What's wrong?' He pushed the screen closer to her line of vision. 'Everything's perfect, Mol. You're perfect.' He snapped a couple of photos, then wiped the gel away and took her into his arms. 'Don't worry, please. That's my job now.'

She managed to clear the slab of emotion crushing her chest, shaking her head with a watery smile. 'I'm not worried,' she reassured him, squeezing him tight to her. 'I'm happy.' She took the photos from the machine, and the pair of them sat on the bed, looking at every detail of the images. Enjoying the moment together.

That night, when they arrived home, Matt put both photos on his fridge, in pride of place. When he took Molly to his bed later in the evening, he grabbed the pictures and tucked them into the frame of a photo of them together on his nightstand.

'We're going to be a family,' he whispered to her before she drifted off, safe and warm in his strong, solid arms. 'I'm going to take care of you both, for ever.'

That was the last thing she heard before sleep claimed her.

We're going to be a family.

She was starting to believe it might all just work out.

After that day, their announcement spread like wildfire. Everyone hid their shock well, and congratulated the pair of them. Molly and Matt settled into life in their new roles. Went to sonograms together, him holding her hand and marvelling at the heartbeat like any new dad would. She found herself nesting at his house, spending any time off work together getting ready for the baby. Relaxing on the couch. Going to see Duncan and Sarah, watching them light up and Sarah get teary-eyed over the baby photos.

It was almost, almost perfect. Her bedroom was barely used; she spent her nights being held in his arms. She felt so close to having the life she'd always wanted, with a man she'd never dreamed of doing it with. As her belly grew, so did her feelings. She tried to ignore the warnings of her shields, make herself wait for the other shoe to drop.

When Amy had said she was moving out, Molly had worried she'd lost her home. Now she thanked God for Anton and his proposal. She and Matt never talked about themselves, their relationship—whatever it was at this point, they didn't make a label for it. She simply waited and hoped. Looked for a sign. But when it came in the form of a phone call the day before they were to leave for his mother's wedding, it was the last thing she'd been expecting. The other shoe suddenly felt like a boot on her neck. Crushing her windpipe, and her foolish misplaced heart.

The tutor running the birthing class that morning was a nice woman named Jessica Sims. Molly had met her a few times over the years, had referred her patients to Jessica's classes. She was one of those earth mother types, always cheerful, patient. Till today.

'Ahem…' She cleared her throat pointedly, and Matt sheepishly took the disposable nappy off his head. He'd been wearing it and pretending to be a toboggan driver, sitting on a foam mat with a rather pregnant Molly in between his legs, twisting their bodies from side to side as if they were heading down an icy slalom.

Molly had been too busy trying to laugh without peeing herself to tell him off. It felt like she had stuffed a bowling ball down her top sometimes, her growing stomach a marvel to them both. Matt couldn't stop touching it, talking to the baby. Touching her, telling her how beautiful she was. How radiant. Even when she developed a craving for pickled onions straight out of the jar, and moaned incessantly every time she tried to get comfortable on the couch, or slide her tired and heavy body into the bath, he'd been there for all of it. Pickled onion runs at midnight? No problem. He'd been there, the whole time…and they were still them. Friends who made each other laugh.

'Sorry.' Matt was contrite, but Molly could see the suppressed mirth in his eyes. 'Do continue.'

Nodding, Jessica resumed the breathing exercises. Matt's hands wrapped around Molly's, and the pair of them breathed and hee-hee-*hoo*-ed together in time with the tutor.

'This is some irony, you know,' he whispered. 'Us learning all this when we could probably teach the class.'

'I know,' Molly said out of the corner of her mouth as Jessica started to demonstrate panting for the head. 'But since you won't have a baby flying out of your hooha in a few weeks, maybe you should count yourself lucky.' Jessica shot him a look that could cut glass. 'Shh, we're going to get told off again.'

'Well, your panting leaves a lot to be desired,' he scoffed, his voice a low rumble in her ear. That rumble ran through her entire body, and she had to remind herself that they were in public. 'You sound constipated.' He made a grunting noise, pulling a face.

Her belly-laugh rang out loud in the room before she could stop it. Jessica was not impressed. Mercifully, they got through the rest of the exercises without further trouble, though she did see a couple of the other fathers crease up when they thought Jessica wasn't watching.

When it was time to practice swaddling the

baby, Jessica gave Matt the only headless doll in the box. 'Sorry, Doctor,' she said. 'Budget cuts, you know. These things cost money.'

Matt took the headless babe without a word, waiting till Jessica was out of his proximity to roll his eyes at Molly.

She took the doll from him and swaddled it in seconds before passing it back to Matt. 'Congratulations, what shall we call him?'

Matt looked serious for a moment, taking in the space where a doll head should have been.

'Headless Hal,' he replied, putting the baby into the sling of his arm and cradling it close.

The fathers all laughed their heads off, the wives rolling their eyes but laughing too.

'Your husband is a handful,' one said to Molly, rubbing her own bump. 'I bet your labour will be hilarious!'

Molly giggled. 'Don't remind me. We're not married. He's…' She hesitated, just for a split second.

'We're best friends,' Matt said, putting the doll on the table and wrapping his arms around Molly from behind, cradling her bump with his hands. He kissed her on the cheek. 'And you're right.' Molly felt him squeeze her a little tighter. 'I am a handful, right, Mol?'

She was saved from answering. Jessica

asked the class to return their dolls and began handing out course feedback sheets for them to complete. She gave theirs to Molly, deliberately avoiding Matt's waiting hand. But all Molly could focus on was the look of surprise the pregnant woman had given her.

We're best friends, he'd said.

From the expression on the woman's face, Molly knew what she was thinking. For the first time in weeks, she felt the bubble walls thin around them. He'd only spoken the truth. It didn't mean she had to like it.

After the class, they'd gone out to lunch, and she'd almost forgotten that look. Matt was his usual self, talking about work, what they had left to do before the baby's arrival. He'd dropped her off at home, and gone to football practice, kissing her like he usually did before she waved him off. She was heading to the bath when she saw the blinking light on his answering machine. She pressed Play and headed for a drink from the fridge, listening to the message. After that, she couldn't stop seeing the pregnant woman's face in her head. *Best friends* rang out loud in her head on repeat.

She listened to the message four more times, and headed up the stairs, all thoughts of a hot bath forgotten.

* * *

The minute Matt walked through the door after football, he knew something was wrong. The air was different.

'Honey, I'm home,' he called, as he'd taken to doing whenever he entered the house. She didn't answer, but he heard movement from the second floor. Moving fast.

'Molly?' he called from the hallway. 'Hello?'

The second he headed up the stairs, towards the noise, and saw her standing in her bedroom, it felt like his breath was being sucked out of his lungs. Her bump was prominent now under her clothing. She looked beautiful, but the way she looked at him nearly knocked him off his feet.

'Molly, what's going on? Where are you going?'

'You don't want this,' Molly spat at him. 'You never did. You said so at the class today—we're best friends. Not some married couple having a kid. I knew I was trapping you by having this baby. I knew it, and God knows I didn't want to. Damn it, it was the last thing I ever wanted. Why would I?' She was crying, the tears streaming down her face. 'I loved my best friend, just as he was. I didn't want to change a thing about him, the same way he didn't want to change me. I should never have told you how I felt that first night.'

'Don't be ridiculous.' Matt took the clothes out of her suitcase as fast as she was putting them in. 'Where the hell is this coming from? I don't regret the baby; I love the baby. You love the baby. I'm glad you told me.'

'Why?' She rounded on him, throwing a pair of socks at him in frustration. 'Why? Why are you glad? You don't feel the same! You never did!' She spotted one of her tops in his hands and snatched it back. 'We should never have slept together. It ruined every-thing!' She threw the top into the case, then tried and failed to get it zipped up. He came over just as she sat down on it.

'Move,' he mumbled. 'Please,' he added when she glared at him. She went to stand, but at this stage in her pregnancy, it wasn't easy. She'd blossomed over the last few months. Bloomed. He'd loved every minute of watching his child grow. He put his hand out, but she slapped it away angrily.

'No. I can do this, on my own.' She flailed like a turtle for what felt like hours, but Matt's hands finally encircled hers, and she was lifted up. He sat her at the edge of the bed, kicking the case underneath.

'I'm still leaving,' she sulked. 'Amy will come and help me pack.'

He was on his knees in front of her, but Molly couldn't bring herself to look at him. If she locked on to those troublesome baby blues, she'd never go. She'd never leave. And she had to. She just had to.

'I don't want you to leave. What's happened?' He sounded so desperate, so disbelieving. 'What don't I know? I left for football practice, and everything was fine!' He was looking around her room, his eyes searching for a reason for her change of heart. She watched him.

How could I have thought any differently?

She realised she was punishing him, but the pain was all hers.

A leopard can't change its spots. He's not to blame.

He'd always told her who he was. She was mad at herself as much as him.

'Victoria called for you today.'

She'd expected his face to fall, his cheeks to blush with embarrassment. A flinch at least but he just looked puzzled.

'Who?'

'Victoria. She left a message. I checked the machine while you were out.'

'Who?' Matt repeated, his brows furrowed over wide eyes.

'Don't,' she warned. 'I'm not stupid, Matt. Victoria. She sounded lovely, said she looked forward to seeing you again after the great day you'd had together.' She felt like a crazy woman, but this was how he made her feel. The minute she'd heard that sweet female voice on the machine, the bubble they'd hidden in for the last few months had popped. They'd slept together every night, but they hadn't had sex for a while. She'd thought his concern about hurting her was over the top, but she'd never considered that he'd been getting it elsewhere.

Stupid idiot.

She watched him, waited for realisation to take hold. It did, but he didn't crumple. He looked almost…relieved.

He is. Her heartbroken mind was talking to her. *It was never going to work. Pull the plug before he does it to you.*

Images of her mother crying flashed into her head. Every time she'd put all her eggs in one basket for a man who ultimately proved not to be worth it. Not to care. To find leaving all too easy. That voice on the answering machine had been a wake-up call for Molly. Amy had said she could stay with her and

Anton, get sorted. She just needed to go, stop the cycle of this heartbreak. He was going to meet someone else, one day. Even if he didn't, he wouldn't be celibate for ever. If he even was now.

'That's why you're leaving?' His voice was a little less desperate. 'Because of a message from a woman?'

'Not just that. Earlier today, at the class!'

Matt frowned. 'The marriage thing?'

'Yes!'

His frown deepened, making him look tense. 'But… I just stepped in. It's no one's business what we are to each other, Mol. We are best friends—that wasn't a lie!'

Molly bit her lip. 'I know that, but the look—' She sighed. 'It doesn't matter anyway. Please, just let me go.'

Matt's hands were on her thighs now as he leaned close to her face, still on his knees.

'I don't want you to leave. And especially not because of some woman. I haven't done anything with anyone since before you moved in.'

'Oh.' Molly wanted to argue the other points, but his revelation had floored her. 'Why?'

His head snapped back in shock. 'Oh, I don't know. Maybe because I slept with my best friend. Had the best sex of my life. After that, I didn't feel the need to go elsewhere.'

He was speaking in sarcastic tones, as if she wasn't getting what he was trying to say. It irked her.

'You don't have to be flippant about it.'

'Flippant?' He laughed, a mirthless, hollow sound. 'I came home to find you packing, crying your eyes out. I'm upset. Why didn't you call me?' His gaze dropped to the full holdall next to her closet. 'Were you just going to leave without telling me first?'

'I—'

'What were you going to do? Leave another note?' He looked around. 'Where is it then?'

'What are you talking about?'

'The note!' He stood and started pacing the room. 'Telling me you're leaving without dealing with the serious stuff. Again.'

The memory of their first night together slammed back into her head. The note she'd left the morning after. She'd escaped then. The memory of it made her cheeks burn. She was escaping now too, but only to protect them both. Again.

'It's not like that.'

He was leaning against the door-jamb now, eyeing her from his cross-armed position. She noticed how bunched his forearm muscles were. He looked as if he was relaxed, but Molly knew he was taut with emotion. He bristled with anger, just below the surface.

'The woman, Victoria? She's the owner of that baby shop we went to the first time. She was ringing because I'd been in again. We still don't have the cot. So I sorted it today, and I asked her to call me when they had some more information about the custom cot bumpers I wanted.'

'It was her?' Molly's spine chilled as she replayed the voice in her head. It hadn't said anything about a date.

You assumed.

She cringed. Feeling foolish. 'I'm sorry. I jumped to conclusions.'

'I understand.' His jaw tightened. 'If I'd heard a message from a man asking for you, I wouldn't have liked it either. There really hasn't been anyone else, Mol. Not since the first time with you. I mean it.'

'Okay,' Molly said slowly, 'but maybe I should move out?'

This time I'd been wrong, she thought to herself. *But next time I might not be. Why wait for it to happen? When I have our child to explain it away to?*

She thought again of her mother, always off with some new love or another.

Will it be the same for us? Me waiting for him at home, dreading the beep of the machine? I can't, won't, live like that again.

Yes, she'd jumped to conclusions on this occasion. It didn't change the facts she would have to face down the line. Eventually, Matt would need to have his own life back, and so would she. This way, perhaps they could still try to salvage the friendship. Raise their child with love. She knew they both wanted that. She pushed down her feelings and brought her shields up high. 'It was only meant to be temporary, staying here with you. The baby and I will have to get our own place eventually anyway.'

'Yeah, well, I don't agree.' Matt was coldly angry. 'You can't just leave without telling me what's really going on. One message from a woman, that's it, and you're jumping ship?'

'I heard you.' This was it. Time to lay all her cards on the table. She needed to tell him as much as she could without revealing her feelings for him. That was what had got her here in the first place. She needed to get out from under all of this, before he ended up hating her. Driving him away was something she couldn't risk. Child or no child, she couldn't live without him in her life. 'The day we found out, about the baby, I heard you talking on the phone to your mum. I tried not to think about it too much, but you don't really want this life, Matt. You never have. The white picket fence idea has always felt like a prison to you.'

'That's...not true.'

'It is.' She reached across the bed for her handbag. Stood to leave. 'I know it is. I know you, Matt, and you will do the honourable thing. Always. I shouldn't have let you. You always do the right thing, and I love you for it—'

She heard him gasp and didn't trust herself to look anywhere near his eyeline. 'I think we had the best intentions, but living and working together, playing house, the baby— it's blurring lines that we just don't need to cross. Not any more.' She put the bag onto her shoulder, standing right in front of him. 'We both need our own lives. I think me moving in with Amy, till I find a place—it's for the best. You can still have your life; I can have mine. We can raise the baby together. Just like before. No courts, no stress. We can raise our child without the need for labels, right?'

'Is that what you really want?' He had moved out of the doorway now, but he was still so close. Searching her eyes, his baby blues roving all over her face. 'Molly, I don't want you to go, but if you're telling me that you really want this, I'll step back.'

'I do want this,' she said firmly, and watched as the light went out in Matt's eyes. He'd dulled visibly before her. She imagined it must have been him seeing the change in her.

We have to stop hurting each other like this.

He'd been looking like this for weeks, so upset at times. So drawn into himself, as if keeping in his truth was just too much for him. What about when the baby arrived? Would the novelty wear off in months, or years? She couldn't be so stupid as to think that he would turn into a monk until their child was eighteen. 'We need our old lives back, Matt, just a little. This way, we can both…breathe.'

She could stop the codependent feelings she'd been having. The fantasy that Matt would declare he loved her too. Like she loved him. As more than a best friend. As the woman, the only woman, he'd ever see his life playing out with. She needed to do this on her own, as she always should have done. Realise her own dream of being a mother, even if her life plan didn't look quite the same as the one she'd had in her head.

'You can't…breathe around me?' He moved aside, his movements clunky till he sank down onto her bed, his legs half collapsing beneath him. 'I never wanted this, Mol.'

'I know,' she said gently.

'Oh, you really don't. You don't have the first clue.' His dull eyes focused on a pink heeled shoe, abandoned on the floor where it had dropped out of her case. 'I'll have your things packed properly and sent to wherever you want. I'll let you get on.' He suddenly stood and walked right past her, his head firmly fixed forward. 'I'll head up to Mum's wedding venue early. Give you some time to move out. I'll pass on your excuses to her.'

She had expected him to go to his room, to go downstairs and pour a Scotch, but he was in and out of his room within moments. She watched as he headed down the stairs, suit bag and suitcase in his hands. The front door shut with a slam, and then she was alone in the house they'd shared.

She sank to the floor and cried her eyes out.

My mother gets married today.

He'd woken in a foul mood and had to keep reminding himself of the fact that it was a happy day. A happy day, which required smiling and pretending to be in a good mood. Even though his life had been completely blown apart and hung around him in tatters. The last thing he felt like doing was grinning at a camera. Watching true love against the odds as Duncan and Sarah promised themselves to each other for the rest of their lives. He hadn't been at his mother's first wedding, for obvious reasons, but he knew how it had ended. The fact Sarah was even looking forward to today was a testament to her strength and resilience, Matt knew. That she could be so happy and eager to live her life with Duncan after what his father did to her. It was maddening. He didn't know why anyone would willingly go through this again. It hurt too much.

Hence the mantra he kept repeating to himself, over and over. Anything to stop him from calling Molly, telling her that he would rather die than see her move out. That the office turned nursery was the best thing he'd ever put together. Better than any operation. Any life he'd saved. He'd loved every minute of the last few short months, and going back to an empty house was just…

He wanted to get in his car and drive straight down the motorway, turn up outside Amy's place and beg Molly to come back with him. To stay in his hotel room, in his bed, be there when he walked his mother down the aisle. To be there after too. Every day after.

It was barely dawn. He'd not done more than doze, despite the half bottle of whisky he'd ordered up to the room the instant he'd arrived. The rest of the night had been a mess of cold showers, unsent texts and angry conversations with his father inside his mind. Matt had declared him dead the minute he'd walked out on them, so why was he bothering to give him head space now? He was lying here, in the hotel room he'd booked to share with Molly, having imaginary discussions with his stupid father. Blaming him for how things had turned out. What was the point? His dad wouldn't give a fig even if Matt did actually tell him how his actions had changed his and Sarah's lives. He was a man who didn't believe in apologies. In looking back. In that last way the two men were similar.

Matt hauled himself out of bed, clad in last night's boxer shorts and feeling more than a little parched after the alcohol the night before. He might as well start getting ready for the day. Distract himself from his phone, the keys to his Lexus that taunted him from the coffee table. After taking a shower, he went over to his suit bag hanging in the wardrobe and pulled the zipper. The second he'd done it, his hands stilled. There was another hanger, a garment placed over the top of his suit jacket and shirt.

'Molly must have put it in there,' he whispered to himself. He reached up to thumb the soft cream cotton. It was a little Babygro with black writing embroidered onto the fabric.

'Grandma's Little Devil,' it said. Obviously a gift from her to his mother. To mark the day. She must have slipped it in there before everything had been so screwed up. Tugging the tiny little item of clothing off its fastener, he held it in his large hands.

Little devil, Sarah said. What if that was true though? After all, the baby was half him. A quarter his father. He went to fold the Babygro up, to tuck it into his suit jacket, but the second he moved the fabric, he heard it. The crinkle of paper.

Molly's note.

His breath rushed out of his lungs, as if she'd just walked into the room. It was a letter written by her, but not addressed to him. It was to their child. From Molly, talking about her and Matt. How they were imperfect but would be there for the baby. She believed in Matt, and the way she wrote about him cracked his heart wide open. The man she described in this letter, to the child they'd made together, stirred him. This man sounded nothing like his father. It did sound like him though.

He thought of everything from the last few months. Molly telling him how she'd seen him that first day they'd met had woken him up. Caused feelings that he'd pushed down and locked away to come knocking again. How had he been so blind? Having Molly as his best friend had brought his humanity back. Molly had been incensed when she'd heard the voicemail from Victoria.

She was jealous.

He'd thought at the time that it was just more proof they couldn't be together because she didn't trust him, but she was jealous. There was a difference. He thought of how he felt whenever he pictured another man in her life. Not just his baby's. Hell, he'd run off enough suitors of hers over the years.

He'd always told himself that he was protecting her. Had gained the skills from being the man of the house way before his time. He realised now why that protective streak towards her had been so ever-present, so strong.

I love her. I want no man touching her, be-

cause I already consider her mine. She belongs with me.

He'd cocked up. She'd probably already moved out of his place, but the letter, the Babygro—they were her way of showing him what she truly felt about him. Even though she'd left him, she'd still wanted him to know how much she trusted him. He hated himself for it. For being so weak he didn't just admit his feelings for her from the get-go. From the minute she'd told him how she'd felt about him that first day they'd met, he'd been running scared. Not from her, but from the words. From saying something he couldn't take back and then letting her down somehow. With the pressure of being so enamoured of her, of so much relying on their relationship now, he'd thought straightaway of his own father, like he always did. Took out the yardstick of his paternal influence, measuring himself against it. But Molly didn't see that. She didn't see *him* like that. The most important revelation that screamed out of the letter was something Matt hadn't expected.

He wasn't his father. Sure, he'd had to grow up in his shadow. People had prejudged him all his life. Assumed he was a bit of a flirt, a womaniser. When he was in medical school and his father was still making waves in the legal world, he'd tried to hide from the name Loren. Instead, he'd made the mistake of damn well living up to it.

'God, I'm an idiot.' He put on his suit, tucked the letter into his pocket and headed for the door. If he got on the road right now, he could still be there and back in time for the wedding. He checked his watch. It would be tight, and his mother would probably have a stroke, but…

He could tell his mum where he was going. To get Molly, to beg her to move back in with him. Into their house, their bed. He wanted to be the man he'd thought he could never be. Molly was the woman all along who saw it in him. Who understood just who he was. She made him *be* a better man. *Want* to be the best man. The version of Matthew Loren that he was when he was with her. He didn't need or want to stay away from her a second longer. He needed to stake his claim on his family in no uncertain terms. *For ever.*

He reached for his phone and dialled her number. After grabbing his keys, he yanked open the hotel door, and heard ringing. Molly was standing there in her maternity bridesmaid dress. She looked like a vision. Pretty in pink. She waggled her cell phone in her hand.

'You rang?'

* * *

Mascara, especially supposed waterproof mascara, was the biggest con women today were sold. Well, the second. The first was that every girl would grow up to meet her Prince Charming. That was a huge pack of lies too. By the time Molly had turned up on the doorstep of where Amy and her fiancé lived, she was a huge snotty mess, streaked with make-up and sobbing into the bag of doughnuts she'd stopped to buy on the way over.

'Hi,' she keened when Amy opened her flat door. 'I brought you wine.' She waggled the bottle at Amy, who took it and brought her inside with a comforting arm. 'The doughnuts are for me, and the baby.' Thinking of her fatherless child made her even worse, and she burst into fresh tears.

They both sagged onto the couch and Amy poured the wine into a glass. 'Anton's working late,' she told her crying friend. 'He sends his love.'

Molly balanced the doughnut bag on her rather pronounced stomach. Amy took a large gulp of wine while Molly sucked the sugar off her fingers, one at a time. She offered a doughnut to Amy, who took it with a grateful smile.

'Where's Matt now?' she asked when

they'd both finished scoffing, and Molly had filled her in on the drama.

Molly shook her head. 'Not sure. I think he went to the hotel. He took his suit. It was awful. I accused him of sleeping around!'

'You reacted,' Amy comforted. 'You're only human.'

'I just didn't recognise her voice. When I heard her, I lost it. I've been stupid to think that he wouldn't be with another woman eventually. I'd hoped…'

'You wanted to be with him, properly.'

Molly just about managed to nod. She needed a second to get over saying it out loud. 'Yep, I know. Because I'm in love with the father of my child, the best friend I have secretly fancied for years. Well, anyway, I made a big scene and started packing my bags. He said he didn't want me to move out, but I was just awful to him. I panicked. I was truly awful, and that was it. I left.'

'He said he didn't want you to leave?' Molly shrugged. 'What did he say about the woman on the machine?

'He knew straightaway who it was. He'd been to the store that day and ordered stuff for the baby. He was really upset, hurt… I think.'

'So, you love him, and by the sound of it he loves you too.'

'Matt doesn't do love. I overheard him talking ages ago. He said that my dream of a family life basically left him cold. I've already exploded his life.'

'Er yeah, and he ran with it.'

Molly looked at her friend, agog.

'Listen, I had my doubts about Matt. But even I can tell he loves you, and he never ran once from your news. He ran towards you, babe. *You're* the one who ran away. Go back. Right now.'

'What, have you not been listening? I've messed it all up.'

'Have you?' Amy gesticulated wildly, sloshing wine onto the couch. 'Okay, no more vino for me. Matt loves you, Molly. It's pretty obvious. All the stuff he's done, your friends saying he's changed. It's for all you, because of you and your baby. You need to sort this out. For God's sake, I am so happy.' She was beaming.

'What are you smiling about?'

Amy laughed. 'You tamed Matthew Loren and turned him into a lovesick puppy. There is hope for women out there, everywhere. Go get him, girl. Now.'

Molly thought of where Matt was right

now, of how long it would take her to get to him. Well, it had already taken years and a confession or two already. Another few hours would be acceptable, if she could guarantee that she could keep him for ever after that. She didn't need the white picket fence. She didn't care about marriage. Hell, she would just rather keep dating her best friend. The father of her child. Or children. Living together, working together, raising their kids and just being them. Tangled in his sheets, and out. She just wanted him. She got up off the couch.

'I need a ride,' she said.

Amy punched the air. 'On it!'

Hours later, and a very anxious drive to the hotel still clinging to her clothing, she was at his door.

'Molly!' His smile was radiant, so bright it near blinded her, but then it was shuttered away. 'Is everything okay, with the baby?'

She touched her bump in reflex. 'The baby is great. I came to see you.'

'Well.' He looked to the floor, and her heart started to sink. 'I was on my way out.'

'Right.'

'To see you. I got your gift.'

'You did, huh?' Realisation spiked the

end of her sentence. 'You were coming to see me?'

'Yes, I realised I didn't want to be any-where without you.'

Molly felt her heart catch. 'So, you were just going to leave your mother's wedding?'

He rubbed the back of his neck with his palm, such an adorable, boyish move. Molly wanted to record it so she could replay it over and over. God, how could she ever have doubted that this man wasn't the one for her?

'Molly, I've...' He took her hand, pulling her into his room. He didn't stop pulling till she was flush against him, his arms coming around her. Caging her, like he always did. She felt so protected and safe in his arms, as if she could do anything. Be anyone, and he'd be right there, watching her. Rooting for her, looking out for her. Their baby was a lucky little one, having this kind of man in their corner. 'I've been trying not to be my father for so long that I ended up being like him anyway. Not telling you how I felt from the start. I'm so sorry.'

'I thought you might feel trapped. When I heard you on the phone...'

'I was talking to my mother and freak-ing out a little, that's all. I wanted the baby. God, I want him or her so bad.' His hand brushed against her stomach, a soft cradle of an embrace. The bump kicked his hand and they both laughed. 'Yes, see?' He was smiling through watery tears, and Molly couldn't take her eyes off his face. His beautiful baby blue eyes had never looked so lovely. Honest, and unfiltered. Just like him.

'I thought I'd trapped you. Any man would be lucky to have you, and here I was knocking you up after one night together, with no ring or promise of one. I felt like a cad, like I'd got you by default. I couldn't handle it, knowing that on the inside I'd be feeling so happy and you'd be looking at your friends, all loved up, and end up hating me.' His features wrestled with an unhappy thought. 'As much as it would have killed me, I'd rather have let you go than break your dreams apart and have you hating me. Listen, I think we could make this work. I—'

Molly put a finger on his lips to stop him talking.

'I don't need any of that. I never did. I don't need a fairy tale, Matt. Life isn't like that, and we both survived our childhoods by learning those lessons. The truth is, the happiest home I ever had was yours.'

Matt pulled her ever closer, trying to speak around her finger. She laughed, taking it away and silencing him with a kiss. He splayed his fingers across her hips, staking his claim on her with his hands, his mouth. When she finally pulled away, he didn't let her go far.

'You mean that? You came to the wedding to try again?' He looked down at her dress. 'You are the sexiest bridesmaid I ever did see.'

She did a mini twirl in front of him. Well, with her current turning circle it was more like a large twirl, but when she saw Matt's appreciative gaze, she'd never felt sexier, more cherished, than she did right now. 'You like? Your mother has excellent taste.'

'Please don't mention my mother right now,' he groaned, reaching for her as he always did and spinning around slowly with her in his arms. 'Especially when I'm plotting approximately ten things I could do to you right now without even crumpling your dress.'

She laughed, watching as he lowered himself to his knees and put his hands around her bump. He looked up at her, and she half swooned. This man, her best friend. He was hers. Finally.

'I didn't write a letter to you, like your mummy did,' he said softly, speaking to the bump but looking straight up at Molly. 'So I thought I would set out my intentions right here. To you both.'

Molly held her breath. She didn't need him to promise anything except to be by her side. That was all she needed. 'Matt, I don't...'

'Let Daddy talk,' he chided, and she pulled a face. He kissed her tummy in response.

'I promise you, right here, on the day of your grandmother's wedding, that I am here. For you both. I love you.' This he said whilst locking eyes with hers, and she felt the pull of him. The delicious shivers his words sent flying around her body. 'I have loved you, always. I will love you, always. I will marry your mummy, commit to you both in every way you want me to. Hell, I will build you a darn white picket fence, and whistle while I work.'

Molly laughed, but realised she was sobbing too. 'No,' she said, after he'd stopped to draw breath. 'No, Matt, I don't need any of that. I don't need the big wedding—hell, I don't need a wedding at all. We did all of this the wrong way around. I mean, who has a baby with their best friend?' She was smiling, and he grinned right back. 'Only us. We have been ignoring what seemingly everyone else around us already knew.'

'True.' Matt muttered something about

Liam. His mother had apparently had a few choice words for him too.

'My point is.' She took his hands in hers and tried to pull him to his feet. He came easily and ended up steadying her. 'I don't need—*we* don't need anything like that. We are not our parents, and we can just love each other and concentrate on that.'

'So, no marriage?'

Molly thought for a long moment about what her dreams had been, before all this. Before the stick had turned pink. She really did have what she wanted. Nothing else was needed.

'Nope.' She wrapped her arms around her love. 'Just this. Just us.'

'Always,' he murmured.

She caught him looking at the clock. 'What's up? Somewhere to be?'

He frowned comically. 'Well, I was supposed to pick up my date…'

She pretended to be offended, wriggling out of his grasp. He took her hands in his, and before she knew it, she was on her back on his bed.

'But…?' she breathed as he came to lie beside her.

'But…' His gaze fell on her lips, and he

bent and kissed her as if he would die if he didn't.

She loved his hunger for her. She had a feeling that he would never lose it. Would always be this desperate to be close to her, as she would be to him.

'The love of my life is here, in my hotel room bed.' He waggled his eyebrows. 'And...' He skimmed his finger along the neckline of her dress, leaving a trail of her goose bumps in his wake. 'We have two hours to kill before we have to leave this room.'

Taking the time to run her fingers through his locks, Molly didn't say a thing. She was too busy enjoying the look on his face. Calm, at peace. Like all his worries had evaporated the second he touched her. She knew because she felt the same.

'Well, Mr Loren,' she said seductively. 'We'd better make them count.'

'Always,' he said, as he got to work on the fastener on her dress. 'I love you.'

And for the next one and a half hours, he showed her just how much he stood by that statement.

EPILOGUE

THE WEDDING DAY was perfect. Utterly, utterly perfect. Molly felt as if she and Matt had committed to each other too. Their vows that had been said in the hotel room, the naughty consummations afterwards, still left a blush on her cheeks and huge admiral butterflies in her stomach. Sarah and Duncan were thrilled to see her there. The pair of them together. When Molly had walked into the side room where the bride was waiting to take her second walk down the aisle, Sarah half screamed with delight.

Molly had walked down the aisle, and watched Sarah come to meet Duncan. Matt was holding his mother by the arm, looking every inch the devilish beast he was. Molly saw a couple of the waiting staff's jaws drop, but she didn't mind. They didn't matter to her and Matt. No woman would ever come between them.

Unless she had another baby, of course. It could be a girl the next time.

She hadn't meant to find out the sex, but when the scans had been done, she'd seen it with her own eyes on the screen. By accident. Their little boy was almost here, and she couldn't wait to see Matt love him too. Like he already did.

Much later that night, they were dancing together. Enjoying the smiles and waves from the other partygoers. She'd always felt like she was part of the Loren family, the good side, and she knew that was cemented now.

Matt had been amazing all day, and though he'd never let on, she'd seen him wipe a tear away when his mother said her vows to Duncan. Sarah had spoken about second chances, how a friendship had blossomed into a great love, quiet and loud in equal measure. About things being just how they were supposed to be in the universe. When Molly had looked across at Matt, she knew that he was thinking the same about them. They'd locked eyes, blue on to blue, and she saw him mouth 'I love you.' She whispered it right back.

She said it to him again now as they swayed together on the dance floor, and the second he heard it his lips were crashing down on hers.

'I love hearing you say that,' he murmured into her ear when he finally let them both come up for air.

'Come on. We always said it. Most days, if I remember rightly.'

His eyes darkened. 'Yeah, but now you know I really do.'

Molly shook her head at him. 'This new tell-all you is going to take some getting used to.'

He cocked an eyebrow. 'Well, we've got time. I take it you're moving back home?'

'That would be a yes, but only on a fifty-fifty basis.'

'Talking numbers isn't half as good as talking dirty,' he quipped. 'I know you're your own person, Molly. Whatever you want. I'll put your name on the mortgage tomorrow. It's ours. His.'

His eyes widened, and she realised what he'd said. He knew the baby was a boy!

'Shoot, Molly— I didn't mean to—'

'You saw it on the scan too! *J'accuse!*' She pulled away, pretending to be indignant with rage and sticking her finger right in his face. He laughed, flicked out his tongue and licked at her digit.

'Nurse Molly Moo, you just ratted yourself out. It's hardly either of our faults.' He grinned. 'Asher.'

'What?'

The music changed, a faster beat kicking in. Their slow sway never changed. Molly saw Sarah smile at her behind Matt and smiled back.

'Not what. Who.'

'The baby?'

'Asher Pritchard Loren. What do you think?' His nervous face was adorable.

God, I adore you.

The fact that he'd been thinking about a name at all should have surprised her, but it didn't. The name was perfect.

'I think it's settled.' She winced as her feet started barking at her. 'And I need to sit down.'

He must have felt her flinch because he rushed to comfort her.

'Chill out, it's only my feet. Stop doctoring me.'

He didn't relax. She could feel it in the muscles of his arm as he took her and led her to their seats at the head table. He said nothing though, silently observing her. She let him. She was fine. She felt great, just tired from the long last-minute drive and the even longer day. She was happy, only with swollen ankles and a heavy head. Putting her feet up on another chair, she tried to get comfortable.

Eventually Matt broke his silence. She ended up answering another twenty questions about her health and begging him not to ask the hotel to bring her a bowl of warm water for her feet in front of everyone. Finally Molly asked him to go and find her a bottle of water. Perhaps a sandwich or two. He looked torn at leaving her side, and it was almost comical. She really did feel fine, and he knew it. His protective streak was back in force, and she basked in it. She was still her, still independent, and this man accepted that. He pushed against it, sure. He turned her on and drove her mad in equal measure. She could go drinking with him, for a game of darts and it would be the best date night in the world. She knew that they'd do just that once the baby came.

Sarah and Duncan had offered to babysit earlier during a chat, and Molly had waited for some sign of discomfort from Matt. The air had changed at first, but then Matt had spoken, directing his words to Duncan, judging by his intent gaze. Those eyes were hard to ignore. Or forget.

'I think babysitting would be great. You will both be the baby's grandparents, after all.'

Duncan welled up, and his mother choked

down what sounded like a little sob of relief. Joy, perhaps. Even Matt's face had flickered, and then instead of shutting down again, he'd grabbed her hand and squeezed. His features had taken on her favourite look, the one where he appeared so serene, happy, unhaunted—if that was even a word. It should be, because it described him perfectly.

'Overnight, weekends,' he was saying, his eyes so warm. 'You might get sick of us calling you. I can't wait to meet our little one, but I am also looking forward to whisking this one off once in a while too.' Molly couldn't wipe the smirk off her face.

'Try to stop us,' Duncan said, coming forward to hug Matt.

The whole day had been filled with moments like these, and the spectre of Matt's father didn't mar the event one bit. Molly had been worried, knowing that Sarah didn't deserve that. Didn't deserve any of it. The same as Matt didn't. She couldn't wait to prove to him over the years just how good he was. She'd fallen in love with her goofy, once-sullen best friend. Head over heels, in every sense of the word, but she was still her. He was still him. They were all in for each other, but their friendship meant that the people they were before were the people they were now, just better together. She had what she'd wanted all along, and what her mother had chased all her life and failed to find.

If Matt's father could see him now, he'd regret his actions. She hoped he would hear that Dr Loren was going places. They both were. Their careers were just as important to them, and their passion would only fuel them all the more. They were already talking about when she was going to return to work. How he could still be a good doctor without losing himself in work like he once did. Just a little snatch of conversation, but they both knew what today signified. Their new life started now. Together, like they'd always been.

When he took her into his arms that night, she knew. With her best friend by her side, she could do anything. She had the fairy tale ending, but in a perfect backwards Matt-and-Molly way. She'd never had to kiss a frog to get her Prince Charming.

The happy ending to her story had been convincing the frog that he'd been a prince the whole time. Her Matt. Her everything. Matt Loren was *home*.

* * * * *

*If you enjoyed this story, check out
these other great reads from
Rachel Dove*

Single Mom's Mistletoe Kiss
Falling for the Village Vet
The Paramedic's Secret Son
Fighting for the Trauma Doc's Heart

All available now!